Breadcrumbs in the Storm

By: Kathy Knight

Look Up Books UK

Copyright © 2014 by Kathleen A Knight

Published by Look Up Books UK
Special Projects, P.O. Box 17, BROMLEY, Kent, BR1 3JP
lookupbooks.uk@gmail.com
www.kathyknight.org

ISBN 978-0-9927931-0-4

All rights reserved. No part of this book may be reproduced, stored in a retrieval system, or transmitted in any form by any means, electronic, mechanical, photocopying, recording, or otherwise, without the prior permission from the copyright owner and author.

Scripture quotations from various translations that include the New American Standard Bible®, copyright © 1960, 1962, 1963, 1968, 1971, 1972, 1973, 1975, 1977, 1995 by The Lockman Foundation. Used by permission. www.lockman.org

Scripture quotations marked (NIV) are taken from the Holy Bible, New International Version®, NIV®. Copyright © 1973, 1978, 1984, 2011 by Biblica, Inc.™ Used by permission of Zondervan. All rights reserved worldwide. www.zondervan.com The "NIV" and "New International Version" are trademarks registered in the United States Patent and Trademark Office by Biblica, Inc.™

Lyrics for 'Praise You in This Storm' written by Mark Hall and Bernie Herms © 2005 Sony ATV Tree Pub: My Refuge Music/EMICMP/Small Stone Media BV, Holland (Adm. by Song Solutions): Word Music LLC (Admin by Song Solutions www.songsolutions.org).
Used by Permission.

Printed and bound in India by
Authentic Media, Secunderabad 500 067, India
E-mail: printing@ombooks.org

Dedicated to

Our two beautifully captivating daughters,
so that through this collection of short stories
you will know God's hand in the passing
of your beloved brother.
May the telling of the Grace of God
be handed down to the generations.

"Don't hide them from your children. Tell the next generation about God's praiseworthy deeds, His power, and His wonders performed."

– Psalm 78:4 –

Psalm 34

This is my chance to praise God; my lungs expand with joyful song. If things aren't going well, hear this story and be at peace. Join me in spreading this news; together let's get the story out.

God met me more than halfway. He freed me from my anxious fears. When I was desperate, I called out and He set up a protection around me while I prayed. God kept an eye on me and His ears pick up even my moans and groans.

Is any one of you crying for help? God's listening, ready to come to your rescue. If your heart is broken, God's right there.

He has been my bodyguard, shielding even my bones. No one who comes to Him loses out.

Paraphrased from 'The Message'[1]

It was after yet another so-called 'coincidence' that my brother said, "This is like following the breadcrumbs."

It was as if someone had laid out a trail of breadcrumbs for a family of tiny birds. They were put out specifically to feed us, comfort us, then lead us out of the raging storm and back home to safety. Like 'manna from heaven', we found ourselves following a path of clues. These led us back home to faith and trust in the Creator God, when He sent us:

Breadcrumbs in the Storm

CONTENTS

Breadcrumbs in the Storm 5
Foreword 7
Preface 9
Prologue 11
1. The Moment That Changed It All 14
2. The Countdown 19
3. The Holiday to Remember 24
4. Gentle Preparation 30
5. Mike, I Love You 34
6. I Want to Go Home 37
7. He's Just Asleep 40
8. The Horn of Gideon 46
9. The Gift of Flowers 48
10. Quiet Times 51
11. Praise you in This Storm 62
12. The Funeral Dress 67
13. Who ate the Biscuits? 72
14. Saved Through Faith 76
15. Pentecost In 50 Days 79
16. The Perfect Number 84
17. I Am Free 88
18. Kutless 94
19. Finding Meaning Among the Rocks 98
20. Overlooking Centre Court 99
21. Leaving the Wilderness With Power 101
22. Mike's Last Day on Earth 107
23. The Lifting of the Cloud 108
24. Public Hearing: Coroner's Inquest 110
Postscript 116
End Notes 118

FOREWORD

Dear Reader!

I believe that you're now holding in your hands one of the more unusual and amazing books to be printed in recent years. Aptly entitled to reflect 'supernatural nourishment' in an extreme crisis, this book holds some extraordinary stories! The events documented here took place over the course of a single month in the life of an everyday family.

My wife Gerda and I first met Kathy, and her husband Mark, in the 1980s. We were Directors for OM Ships International (OMSI) aboard their charity ship, *MV Logos*. Kathy was our Finance Office Supervisor, Mark was our on-board Bookshop Manager, and we were on a unique adventure together taking educational, family and faith books to the developing nations of Central and South America! During those years we became life-long friends. Then, when their children came along, we became God-parents for their son Michael.

As President for the Association of Christian Businessmen in Germany, Austria and Switzerland, I travel far and wide. I meet many people and, in time, I've heard many life-stories of triumphs and tears. So what makes this book so special?

It's the experience of ordinary people who believe and trust in an extraordinary God: the Creator who's continually there with us in the good days, and in the bad days, throughout our lives. The Knight family were trusting this God when something happened in August 2009 that no one could have imagined or prepared themselves for. With busy lives that were actively involved with OMSI, there seemed little warning of what was beyond the horizon for their family.

Kathy had been working in finance at the central hub of OM International, a non-profit organisation with offices in 110 countries. As Area Finance Officer for North Europe, she often travelled to Russia, Ukraine, Poland or the Scandinavian countries. Mark, who was by now Corporate Services Director for OMSI, had been busy with the launch of our newest ship after five years of preparation. Then, suddenly and quite unexpectedly, their eighteen-year-old son, Michael, died in his sleep, without a medical reason why.

Kathy writes here about this shocking mystery in a real, personal, and interesting way. She isn't just documenting what took place over the remaining days of that bizarre month, but she opens up what it meant for them all.

How do you deal with such a tragedy? What goes on in your heart, mind, and soul?

What's different is that the supernatural seemed to step into the natural. So I invite you to take some time now to read their story. Perhaps you too, will take away something for your own life. I am convinced that if you hear the stories that came from this challenging situation, it will open up a whole new possibility: the existence of the God who created you and who takes great interest in your life.

Manfred Schaller

President
The Association of Christian Businessmen
Germany, Austria and Switzerland

Chairman
Board of Directors, OM Ships International

PREFACE

I smiled politely as I gazed into her sincere face. She wasn't the first one to suggest that I write a book after she read my original *Breadcrumbs*. It was a sweet thought, and for that I thanked her. But I'd written the original collection of short stories for personal reasons. With life turned upside down, the faith of our family was turned inside out. So I recorded the stories for our two daughters. They'd lost their beloved brother and now they were looking to us, as their parents, for faith, hope and peace as we searched for a reason why.

Yet another person had suggested that I write. And now I wondered if this was what I was meant to do. But as soon as I 'opened that door', I started to feel sick and muttered, "Does the world need another book? What on earth could I say that is of any use to anyone? The world seems to be flooded with books offering every kind of advice. Is there really room enough for even one more book?"

Then, from somewhere outside myself, I sensed the still, small voice of the Divine. "Yes," He said, "but the world can never have too much personal testimony about ME."

And so you now hold my book in your hands. It's not a 'how to' book of advice or philosophy. It's simply our personal story of what our family has seen, heard and experienced. I want to explore the idea of a Creator God who is not simply some 'nebulous force', but a real person with eyes to see, ears to hear, and arms that reach out to help us.[2]

This book is most especially for a reader who has little knowledge of the 'Maker of Heaven and Earth'. It's for a reader who may be looking for their Maker[3] in perhaps the worst storm they've yet faced.

So to help you understand what I've written, I've added End Notes at the end of this book. You can follow these to find out where my ideas have come from. By looking at the topics or stories I reference in the End Notes, I'm sure you'll take an interesting journey!

When you've finished this book, I invite you to journey on with me in my follow-on book: *Mysterious? ... Expect the Unexpected ...* You'll find it listed on my website. Just click on the page for: *Look Up Books UK*

To take you to a third level still, my *Breadcrumbs* website www.kathyknight.org is there for you to look through. There's family photos and video clips that may be of interest. The tab for *Topics* will take you on a journey of discovery in search of the One who made you in His own image.

For now, I trust that this story here, will become a 'seed of hope' for you that will one day bear fruit in Eternity.

Kathy Knight
breadcrumbslive@gmail.com

PROLOGUE

The state of emergency on the street was intensifying. Our neighbours were running for their cars, clinging to basic belongings that they'd shovelled into their arms. Already a traffic jam had formed on the only exit route from our neighbourhood. My husband, Mark, was away with work and I was home alone with our three kids. But I had no time to think about that now. My focus was on saving our children.

The house shuddered one more time as I raced to the kitchen. Our eldest daughter had been sitting at the kitchen table with her university coursework. I reached the kitchen door in time to see the house foundation break into several large pieces. Lava was rising up from the drains under our street!

Our daughter was on her feet now, standing on an island of molten lava and protected only by a foot-thick cement block. As I grabbed for her with my left hand, I reached for the closest food cupboard on my right. But as I opened the cupboard door, lava poured out onto the disintegrating floor. It had only been minutes, but it was already too late to think about any more supplies.

"Get out! Quickly, get out!" I screamed to the kids who were standing in a back room in a state of absolute shock.

Making our retreat out of town, the children were glued to their car windows. They were pointing in every direction to the rising smoke. It was just like the time of the 2001 *Foot and Mouth* outbreak in the UK. Smoke from the pyres of incinerating livestock could be seen in distant fields. My head was spinning as we joined the exodus on the road heading east.

11

None of us could have believed that our beautiful valley on the border of Scotland would erupt in every direction with volcanic activity! Then I remembered the volcano that our son, Michael, had learnt about a couple of years back. It was in a book that he and I worked on together, and the subject fascinated me.

It was 1943 in Mexico when a farmer saw the ground in his field open up in a 45 metre long crevice. Smoke and fine dust filled the air. Then the ground seemed to swell and rise three metres higher. By the next morning, it was ten metres high and by the end of the day, 35 metres. A modern day volcano was born under their homes! It's called Parícutin (ParicutÃn) after the village it destroyed. Incredibly, it's now 2,800 metres high!

While we jabbered wildly about what we'd learned from Mikey's schoolwork, I fought against the inner panic over Mark being away with work! I could hear a disembodied voice screaming: "I can't do this alone! How on earth are we going to find each other in all this chaos?"

But the nightmare was only just beginning.

The road we were on meets a main 'A' road to the east coast of England. This was our only hope of escape. But as we rounded the corner and entered a level stretch, the landscape spread out to reveal rising smoke. It came from a smouldering river of lava that had opened up where the main junction used to be. By now, our house was sure to have been destroyed. There would be no chance of retreat returning back by that route. Now the road ahead was completely cut off! The kids were whimpering and my blood ran cold.

✷ ✷ ✷

I opened my eyes and looked out of our bedroom window. A pale streak of winter sunlight was gathering on the south-eastern horizon. It could be seen through the condensation that had formed behind the curtains during the night.

I snuggled deep into the blankets, tucking them firmly round my back and cold neck. Then I pushed back the vivid imagery of that unwanted dream.

… It was New Year's Day 2009.

1. THE MOMENT THAT CHANGED IT ALL

It seemed to be an ordinary mid-summer Saturday morning. The sun was shining through our large bedroom windows that overlook our south-facing back garden (an important house feature in the borderlands between Scotland and England where sunshine can be a rarity). Unbeknown to me, as I made my lazy exit from our bed, I'd just woken to a morning that would bring irreversible change to our lives, and to the history of our little family from that point on.

We had been living in the UK for 15 years and working with the non-profit organisation OM Ships International (OMSI). Mark had begun work with OMSI in 1979 and I had joined the charity from Australia back in the early nineteen-eighties. We met each other while working aboard OMSI's smallest ship, the *MV Logos*, in Venezuela, South America. With a million visitors a year coming up their gangways, the idea was to bring *knowledge, help and hope* to developing nations. This was done through the voluntary crew and staff and through the literature that was sold in the large on-board bookshop.

After leaving our life on the high seas, we'd been based at the International office on the border of Scotland and working with the logistics and organisational side. OMSI had two ships in action at the time and we were also standing at the finish line of a massive five-year project renovating another much larger ship.

On August 1st 2009, Mark had woken around 7 a.m. He had made a cup of tea and had returned to bed. While I enjoyed snuggling deeper into the blankets on that Saturday morning, Mark fired up his laptop.

15

Our oldest daughter was at sea at the time. She was a staff member aboard the newest ship that OMSI had recently launched. She was visiting several ports in the Caribbean. Our youngest daughter had made her bed on the floor of her room that night, and was still asleep there behind her closed door.

But just after 8 a.m., Mark got concerned for Michael — our middle child and only son — who hadn't yet risen for work.

For close on a year, Michael had been working as a "hamburger chef"[4] for McDonalds. Before that, he'd been a short-term volunteer also with OMSI. Preceding his older sister, Mike had spent six months visiting nine countries in the Caribbean, while working as a deckhand aboard the OMSI ship, *Logos II*.

But Mike came home firmly set on a future in Gospel music — 'good news' songs written about the Creator God and His Word. He wanted to be one of those people who lead the music in Believer's meetings. Perhaps he may have had the privilege of playing his guitar one day at a large-scale Gospel music event. The idea was to raise as much money as he could from his wages at McDonalds (as well as through sponsorship from kind friends and family) to put himself through a college course at a Music School in Coventry.

At eighteen, Mike was self-sufficient. He often left the house before the rest of us had risen. But that morning, he hadn't stirred yet for his 9 a.m. shift. So Mark decided to wake him.

There was no response as Mark stood in the darkened doorway. He turned on the light and called to Mike again. He was lying in a completely relaxed position as if deep in sleep. His hands rested half-open on his pillow beside his face and his right knee could be seen at the side of his rumpled duvet. But there was something clearly wrong!

Going over to his bed, Mark gave Michael a kind of arms-length gentle shake. Instantly, he knew without doubt that our son (our only son whom we loved, in him we were well-pleased[5]) ... was dead.

Emerging leisurely from our bedroom, I met Mark on the landing. He was holding the banister rail and gasping for breath. "I'm not joking," he said. "Call 999. Mike's dead."

It seemed that I stepped out of my body at that point. For close on three months following that one life-changing moment, I lived and moved in some bizarre out-of-body, fragmented state of existence. As if either one inch ahead of my body or else one inch behind my soul.

I pushed past Mark on the landing and headed straight for Mike's room. I stood over our boy, clutching my hands and taking in his fractionally opened eyes, and lips that had already begun to turn white. I could hear my disembodied voice saying, "Yes, he's gone. He's definitely gone."

In a surreal limbo, I was abnormally calm. It was as if I'd been hit by a car, thrown into a hedge, picked myself up, and stood on the sidewalk staring into space and saying I was fine. This was clearly not a rescue situation. You don't get white lips, even partially white lips, in three minutes. After four minutes you can have irreversible brain damage. Mike had been gone much longer than a rescue could reverse.

I *walked* down the steps, went to the phone, and dialled 999. Then I whispered, "God, what are you doing? You're up to something. I know you're up to something. What are you doing? You have to tell us what you're doing!"

The operator had answered by the time I reached Mark, and with dreamlike composure I simply said, "I'll pass you over to my husband." Then I returned to Mike.

17

Less than two minutes had passed from the time I got out of bed that sunny Saturday morning. Two short minutes, in which a tsunami engulfed our home, leaving one of us dead.

Two minutes for a volcano to erupt in unthinkable power right under our feet. In a metaphoric way, and just as it was in my New Year's dream, it was as if lava had begun to push up through the floor boards and flow out from every cupboard. This was a volcano that would rock our home and surely split apart our foundation stones.

There was no warning and no time to gather supplies for the long journey ahead. It was as if 'personified devastation' had encamped in every direction around us while we tried to escape.

There was no chance at all of retreat down yesterday's road.

★★★

The following is a story that took place during the remaining days of August 2009 — the days that followed those two infamous minutes. It's the story of what happened to our family after the sudden, unexpected and unexplained death of our eighteen-year-old son. With our world turned upside down our lives were turned inside out. But HOPE returned, after encountering what we can only describe as 'supernatural coincidences' in the days that followed.

Due to the uniqueness of all other personal stories, our story is likely to be non-transferrable for the most part. It's a story of unearthly compassion that seemed to be laid out on our life-path like *breadcrumbs* to follow. It's about 'treasures of darkness' that we found stored for us in secret places.[6]

In an extreme crisis, this story opens up the concept of the existence and involvement of the Creator God, who created and sustains all things.[7] We've found, in our own story, that He's alive today and actively involved in the Story of Life. What our family has experienced has caused us to see how Father God is at work in minute detail and He's revealing His love to ordinary people in extraordinary ways.

2. THE COUNTDOWN

The countdown for Mike's departure could be dated back to January 2009, when my brother, Bill, stepped through the doors of a travel agent in Australia and asked for a flight to the UK. One was chosen for Sunday morning August 2nd. He and his wife, Lorna, had never taken holidays in August, and why August 2nd? But right up to Saturday August 1st he had no idea why they were going to England, apart from having a desire to 'be available' for whatever God had planned for them — whatever that meant.

It could be said that the days intended for our boy were written in God's 'book of life' when He knitted Mike together in my womb.[8] With his days embedded into his DNA code, His Maker watched him enjoying each birthday, knowing it was one year closer to the finish line. Then, God knew when I said goodnight (and managed to sneak a kiss on Mike's neck as he sat watching TV on July 31st) that I wouldn't again get that privilege. To feel Mike's warm skin against my face and smile as he wriggled from my embrace.

After learning that the Creator God is all-knowing (omniscient), I felt sure that God knew the day and the hour that Mike was to leave this earth. In our summer newsletter, concerning the recent death of our close friend in Australia (and sent out just days before Mikey left us), I wrote:

"The deepest questions in life aren't answered when searching through what we **don't** know, but in what we **do** know. We know that God knows our days from our birth. A time frame is given to us all. What we do in that time doesn't give us a right to an extension in the 'eleventh hour'...

...Instead, it serves to make us proud of how we lived for our Maker, while we had the time."

The days designed for Mike were eighteen years, six months, twelve days and somewhere within 24 hours. That's 222½ months; 967 weeks or 6,769 days. He was born on a Saturday morning and he died on a Saturday morning.

God knew — but He didn't warn us.

Due to suspected epilepsy when Mike was younger, we had his heart tested at a specialised heart unit on the east coast. Yet we still weren't alerted by the doctors to any problems that could one day end his life.

Some friends told us about a genetic disorder that kills even the most athletic of young people, but that still doesn't explain why God kept quiet! Even when Mike stopped breathing in the early hours of August 1st, we slept soundly. We had no prompting from this Lord of Life that would bring us to his room to save him.

With tears that blurred my vision and made my heart ache, I sat in bed late one night stroking the picture of Mike's smiling face. He was looking up at me from the cover of his funeral service program. I was struck then by the fact that God knew when that picture was taken (in the year before), that I would one day weep for that lost smile.

It would be a smile that will only ever be enjoyed now from a computer screen or a cold paper printout. The paper, like thick glass, separates me from Mikey now. How I wished in that darkened room to find a secret door to step through that paper into Mike's world. If only for only a short time, to hug him once more. To tell him how proud I am of him, and to say goodbye.

My finite mind was swimming in speculation. I rushed headlong toward pure physical answers. These could topple my frail stack of 'faith cards' that I'd piled high around my confused heart. Pure logic told me that Mike's dead, plain and simple. The machine stopped, that's it and that's all. Death happens all the time and 100 percent of humankind will experience it for themselves at some point.

Then I'd swing toward 'divine precepts' that dreamed of Mike in worship before the throne of God.[9] Mike left for 'a higher calling' and greater purpose. As the sun rose on August 1st 2009, Mike was visited by The Bridegroom Himself.[10] He was collected in just the same way that the Angels took Lot by the hand and resolutely led him and his family out of the city of Sodom almost four millennia ago.[11] Or, like Enoch in the *Book of Genesis* in the Bible, Michael *"...walked with God. Then he was no more, because God took him away."*[12]

In the days following August 1st my mind travelled far and wide over what on earth happened to Mike and why we weren't warned. Then the voice of King Solomon's Wisdom seemed to float past me: "Speculation, speculation! All this is speculation."[13] The logic of it snapped me back to reality. It's meaningless to speculate over things that can't help.

The fact is: the Creator God is above being answerable to me, just as He was above being answerable to Job in the Bible.[14]

The fact is: God will be God in heaven as He has always been on earth. Although I may come one day into my Maker's presence and be changed, purified and even 'holy'[15], God will still be God. As such, He will continue to remain above being answerable to me.

The fact is: Even in heaven (and contrary to the kind words of our friends over this time) I *may never know why* this has happened.

The reason that we *may never know why* is because God is God and His sovereign authority rules. There has never been a day, nor will there be (even until the end of time), where it will become necessary for the Creator of Heaven and Earth to explain His actions to a created being (transformed and holy though I may be when I see Him face-to-face) because, quite simply and yet quite completely ... He ... is ... God.

Having said that, and while He didn't warn us, it isn't true to say God did nothing about it. Quite the contrary, the *breadcrumbs* we've followed in this storm have been sweet, honey tasting "manna"[16] that feed our parched souls on this storm-filled journey. But to understand what I am saying throughout this book when I talk about *breadcrumbs* or *manna,* let me tell you about a story from the Bible.

Between three and four millennia ago and before Israel became a nation, they were a people group who lived as slaves in Egypt. In a decision known only to Himself, the Creator God chose this family to dramatize His epic story for the world, through the Bible. The *Book of Exodus* in the Bible shows how Father God rescued Israel from slavery, then provided for them and fed them for 40 years in a Middle Eastern desert. Their food was an unusual wafer like *breadcrumbs* that appeared with the dew each morning.

It tasted like wafer made with honey but they didn't know what to call it. They ended up calling it "manna" which means: *"What is it?"* Wherever they went in those long wilderness years, they had *'manna from heaven'* and it stopped appearing three days after they arrived at their destination.

★ ★ ★

Our own *breadcrumbs* — our 'manna from heaven' — on this personal road to recovery were unexpected discoveries and 'food for thought' for us. These moments seemed to nourish our souls. They helped us to put one foot in front of another on a journey back from sinking sand to solid ground.

And so it has been that the 'collective whole' of Mikey's story (that crossed him over from life to LIFE) seemed to us to be none other than a God-given, loving-filled act, not only toward Mike, but also to those he left behind. These supernatural coincidences have shown us that Mike's Maker was, and is, involved in the intimate details of what has now become His story in our family's history.

3. THE HOLIDAY TO REMEMBER

It was January of 2009 and they had only just returned home from a beach holiday when, quite unusually, my brother Bill and his wife, Lorna, sat down at their computer to plan a trip to the UK. I say *unusually* because it isn't the normal behaviour of anyone to come home from a relaxing holiday only to plan the next one so soon. Surely you would wait for the fatigue of work to settle in before your mind begins to daydream again of some distant shore.

On this occasion, the thought to go to England began on a Saturday and by Wednesday the tickets were booked to leave on August 2nd. In their minds though, this trip was special. From the outset, they felt strongly that this was a different trip. Both he and Lorna were to be available to 'follow God's lead' — whatever *that* meant.

I had left Australia 25 years before and this was the first time that my brother had made a trip to visit me so, of course, I was excited. I wrote a long email in response and outlined all the places that they should go while they were here.

But I was somewhat deflated when he responded with not wanting to plan anything. From the beginning there seemed to be 'an unknown element' to their plans for visiting England. So they wanted a free diary to 'be available' for whatever it was that God should put before them.

Six weeks after booking their trip to see me, Bill had a dream. It was the sort of dream that he hadn't had before, nor has he had one like it since. In his dream, he saw a raging storm with three tornados and it came without warning.

Although Bill was on high ground, the storm cones surrounded him and peppered him with debris. From where he stood he could see a storm surge on lower ground that almost drowned his family. After it died down, he tried to understand it but had no answers. This angered him greatly and he turned his anger toward Lorna. When Bill woke up, he wrote down what he saw.

It was March 2009.

In June my church friends in Australia experienced a real setback. The lady responsible for the care of missionaries in our church had moved Missions Month from April to June, without an explanation why. She was then diagnosed with cancer and passed away in early June. As their longest serving overseas worker, my Pastor recalled me home.

I stayed with Bill and Lorna for the remaining weeks of their Missions Month and flew back to the UK in early July.

Coincidentally (though I now wonder about all coincidences in my Maker's storyline for my life), it was 25 years to the very month that my church family had first prayed for me and sent me away back in 1984. They have faithfully sponsored us financially since then, for the charity work we've been doing with OMSI.

But unbeknown to me, my brother was secretly disappointed to see me! He'd spent all that money on a trip to England leaving on August 2nd, and I was sitting in his kitchen in June! He had clearly misheard God and wondered if God was even in the plans to travel in the first place?

In consolation, he reasoned to himself that God surely would have known back in January (when he set about booking a flight for August) that I would be coming home in June!

With this unfolding, he relented and booked some small sight-seeing items of interest for the first week that they would be in the UK. They then hired a car to circle the south, before coming to me on August 10th.

On the Sunday before they were due to fly out, close friends asked Bill if he was excited about the trip. But He simply replied that he didn't know how he felt and wasn't sure how the trip would go. Because of the uneasy feeling surrounding the plans in the months before, this unusual lack of excitement seemed to play on my brother's melancholy tendencies. By Saturday August 1st (Friday night, UK time), he wondered if he and Lorna may die on the trip.

In preparation, he called his sons over on Saturday afternoon. While the clock ticked on to the early hours of Saturday morning in England, he laid out on the kitchen table instructions concerning their Will and other things to explain to their sons and daughter-in-law.

As evening approached (and now drawing close to 8 a.m. UK time on August 1st), Bill was still dragging his feet. He was packing the remains of a suitcase less than 15 hours before they were due to leave for the airport. Since there was a ladies meeting at a friend's house that night, Bill suggested that Lorna attend that group while he finished the last few tasks.

However, in a phone call with one of our sisters, he still couldn't explain what was wrong with his attitude. He could only say later, that 'the thrill was missing' from what should have been an exciting first-time adventure to our ancestral homeland.

Just as he placed their packed suitcases and tickets by the front door, his phone rang. It was then that he understood the true nature of this long-awaited trip.

Our Mum explained that Mark had found our Michael dead at 8:05 a.m. (5:05 p.m. Australian time). Instantly, my brother knew that this trip, which had been in the pipeline and seemingly under God's direction since January, was the reason and true purpose all along. As head of the home and father figure since our father's death 10 years before, God knew my brother's place was at my side.

Lorna had only just walked in the door at the ladies group when her mobile phone rang. To the bewilderment of everyone, and not explaining it even to her, Bill simply asked her to return home. When she returned, it took Bill several minutes out on the driveway to get the words out. After reading the manuscript for this book, Bill wrote:

"I can still clearly remember those horrible words. It was just like the time when I told Lorna that her Dad was dead. I said, 'Mark's just rung from England! Michael's dead. Their son Michael — they've just found him. I've just spoken to Mark on the phone. Mike was still in bed ... Michael's dead.'"

Both of them knew immediately that this was Father God's plan for them all along: to be with me in this dark storm.

However, it took five more years, and the reading of the manuscript to this book, before Bill connected his storm dream (that peppered him and Lorna with debris), to my own life-storm. So when I received his story by email, I simply had to include it here before the book went to print.

Several things about the dream proved to be true. When life-storms hit in any form, they'll often come unexpectedly. The shock causes numbness and denial. The intense outbreak will often engulf or surround you on every side. The resulting disorientation causes confusion, sleepless nights, depression, withdrawal, apathy and a feeling of unreality.

The life-storms that hit with unthinkable intensity are likely to split into several significant parts. These issues will often head in different directions and will have to be tackled separately. The result is increased shock that causes crying, lost appetite, self-criticism, guilt and various physical symptoms (mostly related with your heart and stomach).

The problem with being peppered with debris from every direction (as Bill's dream showed), is that you won't be able to see clearly. You'll therefore struggle to find the answers that you're looking for. Most certainly the emotional rollercoaster through this confusion can bring on anger and even rage. It'll almost certainly be vented against those closest to you such as your spouse — those who themselves are being peppered with the same debris that you are.

But rather than experiencing calm after the high-level storm hits, a storm-surge at ground level (as his dream showed) is likely to flood in to drown those you love most.

So in the immediate days that followed Mike's death, a good friend (who had gone through the storm ahead of us with the loss of their little girl) regularly phoned Mark and stood watch in prayer for our marriage. With the solid ground washed out from under our feet, some statistics show that as many as eight in every ten families who lose a child, may go on to suffer a divorce as a result.

In the immediate hours after our storm hit though, we didn't know any of the significant elements in Bill's dream. We could, however, see that Father God was moving those closest to us into place before our own private tornado fell upon us. Even the seemingly insignificant details seemed to fall neatly into place. With one hour of Sunday trading time before they were due at the airport, Bill was able to completely reverse the plans that they'd booked and paid for months earlier.

Then they got a mirror image of the original itinerary at no extra cost. This put them in the north with me in the first weeks of August and in the south of England for their remaining week before flying home. The ease with which all this fell into place with no detriment to any of the original plans (apart from the cost of an upgrade to a last-minute internal flight) was little short of a miracle!

After stowing their hand luggage in the over-head bins above them on the plane, they buckled up into their seatbelts in preparation for the whirlwind that was to follow — yet knowing that they were in the centre of God's Will for their lives.

4. GENTLE PREPARATION

Mark had just come off the largest project in our charity's 50-year history. By April 2009 he was tired of faith. Sitting on deck aboard OMSI's ship, the *Logos Hope,* Mark was complaining to God over the lack of resources and personnel. He wrote: "30 years with OMSI this October. Toughest year: the last 12 months."

As he looked out over the millpond haven of Leith harbor, Edinburgh, he complained to himself over why charitable or 'faith projects' couldn't be smooth sailing and easier. Then he imagined the currents and waves, the bad weather and the great highs that are almost certainly followed by the deep lows. All of this was just beyond those harbor walls.

In a split second, he felt sure that Father God had responded to him with a question: "Do you want a life that's safe, or an adventure of faith?"

Over the next days, Mark searched the Bible for what God may have meant by this question. The notes that he formulated became a sort of 'personal life message' that he used for himself and when talking with others over the next months: "If I live an adventure of faith, I'll be living in the 'Reality of the Kingdom'. If I live a life that's safe, I'll only be living with the 'Concepts of the Kingdom'."

After looking through the *Book of Hebrews* in the Bible, Mark noticed that Chapter 11 had listed those who lived the adventure of faith, not a life that's safe. So he wrote: "They lived in the 'Reality of the Kingdom'. What does that look like? Enoch walked with God. Walking is different to talking." He then listed moments that the leadership of OMSI had 'walked through' along with some key words.

The list showed both the good and the bad that were coupled with polarized emotions along the way. Then he wrote something that, although written to process work related issues, was to become a challenge for us when our new reality (with drastically reduced emotional resources) began for us:

"Is your vision (your ability to perceive what's set before you) greater than the natural reality and your resources?"

The project of renovating a large North Sea ferry that had accommodated 1,000 passengers for a three-day voyage, to a permanent home for 450 crew and staff was a real feat!

As Director for the Corporate Services division, Mark's responsibility was to ensure that all future business services for the community on board were built into the renovation changes. If the ship was a nine-floor office block, what would be needed? So this included systems and the location of the administration areas with associated needs e.g. IT, satellite communications, AV needs throughout the ship (as well as in the main conference room and the 450-seat *Hope Theatre* on board), and the security badge system for staff.

With 25 years of experience in OMSI's Literature division, Mark also headed up the design of the book holds and onboard bookshop deck — now the largest floating bookshop in the world that receives a million guests every year. For two of the recent years, Mark had also been overseeing the finance systems for OMSI. At that time, this included three ships.

Metaphorically, it had been a long 10-year 'marathon' and by late July, Mark had sensed that he'd made it to the finish line. Now launched into her future, the *Logos Hope* would be carrying *knowledge, help and hope to the people of the world* and … our oldest daughter sailed away with them.

32

When the ship left the UK, and after coming home from the following board and leadership meetings that week, Mark looked back at the cost in completing the project. He now had time in our quiet house to reflect on the close of this epic venture: the personal price paid; the loss of his boss and close friend; the dissipation of a once strong project team, and the natural moving on of some key leaders — some of these had worked with Mark for 30 years.

On Friday afternoon, July 31st, he wrote a personal email to close friends from the original Executive Leadership Team (ELT) — men who had also 'endured the heat' of that massive endeavour. In one last email before shutting down his computer and coming home he wrote these words:

"I realised in the last two weeks that I'm going through a mourning process and that 'the death' was both sudden and unexpected."

It seemed very clear that the end of both the project and the composition of the ELT as it was, marked the end of something far bigger than just the end of a joint mission. During that week Mark sent me a list of all the necessary information for accessing our bank files, and where our family finance stood. He thought something serious was going to happen to *him*.

This was a hard 'breadcrumb' to swallow as the events of the following morning unfolded. Waking up that sunny Saturday morning to find that our only son had passed away in the hour before we found him, was surreal to say the very least — especially in light of the choice of words in Mark's last email.

But if that was mere coincidence and not ironic in itself, four years after our greatest storm, Mark found the notes that he'd written down back in April 2009.

33

The incredibly fitting notations (including the fact that we had no emotional 'resources' for our new 'natural reality'), coupled with the things that Mark had been working through in his own mind during the months before August 2009, confirmed something in us: *The God Who Knows all Things* had been laying a foundation for us to stand on.

In the minutes after Mark found Mikey, Enoch in the Bible came to mind. We had Enoch's Bible verse about 'walking with God' put onto Mikey's tombstone. Four years later, we found that Enoch was part of Mark's notes from April 2009.

This, and my brother's story in Chapter Three, has shown me that Father God seemed to give insight (through His Holy Spirit at work within them) to the two most important men in my life. Even if it was received as 'a shadowy vibe'. Even with it being like fragmented clues, that couldn't be crystallised until the whole truth was known in the hours that were to come.

At the time of perhaps my greatest need yet, I knew that God was at work in the painful events of both life and labour, showing us His knowledge, enduring presence and sovereign hand of control … even in the storm.

5. MIKE, I LOVE YOU

It was after 10:30pm on July 31st when I kissed Mike goodnight before I headed to bed. His younger sister, Laura, was still pottering about and eventually went to the kitchen for a drink of water. Mike was still awake and down stairs too. When Laura was leaving the kitchen, however, she got an overwhelming sense inside. She felt sure that she should tell Mike that she loved him.

At first she thought that this would be awkward. Sisters don't tell their brothers that they love them — do they? As the room went into slow-motion then seemed to pause for a moment in time, she remembered thinking, "This moment is passing." But then she knew the moment had passed.

Instead she said, "Don't forget to turn off the light, Mike."

By the time she reached her room she was overwhelmed with emotion. She decided to make a bed on the floor that night where she began to cry. She didn't know what she was crying about as she sobbed quietly to herself in the dark. But one word came to mind: the word 'lonely'.

The next thing, she woke up and it was morning. She could hear Mark saying to me, "Kath, I'm not joking. Call 999. Mike's dead." It was then that she realized what had happened to her the night before. Laura stayed in her make-shift bed until after the ambulance crew arrived. She spent those minutes in tears and listening to what was happening outside her door.

During that morning, her key question was, "Do you think Mikey knew that we loved him?"

35

Though it took her another couple of months to tell us her story, I quietened her fears that morning with an unreserved, "Yes!" Even when sisters annoy their brothers, underneath it all, they will always know they're loved.

As we sat quietly with Mike's body, while the medic wrote his notes, Laura told me a story that happened at school:

Just before the summer holidays began, her English class was covering the story of Romeo and Juliet. Laura had been put off by the idea having an open casket in the family home where relatives came to pay their respects. Laura sat in class wondering what it would be like to be in the same room with a dead body. She told her friends that she would never be able to even look at a dead body. However, within a few weeks, she was sitting next to the body of her only brother.

With Mike at rest on his pillow so peacefully, he looked as if he was asleep so it didn't frighten her at all. When I left the room to phone Mikey's work to tell them what had happened, Laura sang him a Matt Redman song *The Heart of Worship*. It was a lovely gesture for a little sister, especially considering the lyrics along with Mike's hopes and dreams to become part of something bigger than himself — something in honour of His Maker.

The house, and our lives, went into overload for the next days and months as Laura tried to settle into school again. But it seemed that Father God knew her feelings of hidden guilt and in His time, this issue needed to be addressed.

Four months after her brother died, Laura had a dream. In her dream she was walking down our street. She came to a familiar spot where Mike stood waiting for her. As she came close to him she said, "I love you, Mike." He turned and began to walk away but Mike turned back and said, "I love you too." ... Then he was gone.

The next day, Laura told us about her hidden burden. In tears of amazement and thankfulness, she recounted her dream. We were all sure that Father God knew that such hidden pain would only fester and become worse in time. By seeing this dream, Laura was not only happy to share with us what she had buried at the back of her heart, but it was also as if she'd been given a second chance. She knew that Mike knew just how much she loved him. Now she knew he had always loved her too.

Incredibly, Laura was also able to have this story filmed in 2012. The three-minute clip has since been shown in several countries including being translated into Portuguese for a Brazilian TV channel. You can see this film clip on the *Videos* page of my website www.kathyknight.org

When Laura finished school and went to Africa for a year, she designed a pull-out story card about the size of a credit card. It's her story. She would give this card away to people that she happened to meet on the streets of Cape Town. She titled it: *God Give's Second Chances.*

6. I WANT TO GO HOME

Set in one of the most beautiful parts of the English countryside, the convention is an annual gathering right at the heart of the idyllic Cumbrian Lake District. Away from the hustle and bustle of city life, the combination of retreat time, gospel music, topics discussed, and the youth camp programs, have been a real 'refreshment time' for so many over the past 150 years.

Win and Peter made this a yearly event in their family calendar. And since Peter was the chairman of the convention's Trust, he took responsibility each year for the Guest Speakers. On the final Saturday of each year's event, it was his usual practice to stay until the last of the key note speakers left town. He wanted to ensure their travel arrangements ran smoothly, and that the start of their homeward journey (after an often tiring week for them), began without 'hiccup'.

However, as the 2009 summer convention drew to a close, Win began to experience an increasing urgency to go home. By Friday July 31st, this inner feeling was so strong that Win just had to share it with Peter. She didn't know why she was feeling this way. It was completely out-of-the-ordinary for her and quite illogical.

With only 12 extra hours to wait, Win was feeling incredibly silly and couldn't explain the urgency in the need to leave. She was happy for Peter to stay on for his guests, but she simply had to go home!

Analyzing it later, Win acknowledged that she had a very good week. So it was nothing to do with the meetings, the crowds, or even being tired.

38

It was more of an ever-present (and growing) sentiment that was by now *compelling her* to skip their usual Saturday afternoon plans and to return home after the last meeting on the Friday night.

Slightly reluctantly, Peter consented to leave as well. So, for the first time ever, he decided to say goodbye to those invited for key roles, then he joined Win for their early return back home. But it wasn't until Peter answered the phone at 8:20am the following morning, that they both grasped the full impact for a need to return home.

It was Saturday morning August 1st 2009, and Peter was the first person Mark had called after the medics pronounced Mikey dead. Peter and Win's response was immediate.

Had they remained at the convention, I'm sure that their response time would have only differed by 45 minutes. It was heartwarming though, to see their faces at our front door in less than 10 minutes! Peter was able to take control of the situation after Mark's initial calls to our two mothers. While Win made us a cup of tea, Peter was able to make all further phone calls necessary. The worst of these was to our ship.

Mike's oldest sister was at sea at the time volunteering with OMSI as a staff member aboard *Logos Hope*, which was berthed in St Vincent in the Caribbean at the time. Our ship's Director had the task of breaking the news to her. That her tall, healthy, strong brother was unexpectedly, and quite mysteriously, taken from her without a reason why.

Win's growing unease as the week progressed, and Peter's choice to join her at home earlier than planned, was something neither had experienced in all the years that they'd been involved in such a significant annual convention. We can only think now that Father God was speaking into their hearts.

39

Father God seemed to be moving Win and Peter into place like a coast guard life boat, ready for the moment the 'white squall' smashed into our quiet lives. When all the incoming calls began, Peter provided an initial buffer for us. At one stage that morning all four phones (in addition to Peter's personal mobile) seemed to be 'ringing off the hook'!

Their compassionate and calming presence that day was like a life ring thrown out to us from the decks of a passing ship, plucking us from a raging sea.

If August 1st 2009 was a scene unfolding from Life's dramatic Play, it was as if the stage had been lit with filtered lighting that beamed down from the 'Goodness of God'. This may seem hard to believe right after this same God stopped sustaining our son, our only son whom we loved, and for no apparent reason at all. Nevertheless we encountered extraordinary coincidences throughout the remaining 30 days of August 2009 — supernatural *breadcrumbs* that seemed to be laid out for us on our path.

Like tiny birds feeding on what the mother bird provided, these ironic moments have demonstrated Father God's love to us. Through them all, we've tasted a little of what one ancient king meant when he said: *"Because Your love is better than life, my lips will praise You."*[17]

7. HE'S JUST ASLEEP

The police woman attending the scene came off her two-way radio and warned us that they were about to take Mike's body. If we wanted to get some time with him, she suggested that we should do it now. But Mark didn't want to 'see him like that', so I went to Mike's room to say goodbye alone.

Earlier, the emergency services had asked us to lift Mikey down off his bed and onto the carpeted floor. We were to give him heart massage until the ambulance arrived. Mikey lay at peace on the floor now, under his duvet. I had placed his stuffed dog, Ro-Ro, on the pillow beside him.

When I entered the room, I knelt down on the floor next to him. Then, just like people in the Bible like Hannah or Job, with my head on the floor, I was determined to worship the God who gives and who takes away:

"For Mike's sake. For the sake of the worship that he had his sights set on. I will be like Job and worship the God who gives and takes away — right here, right now. I'm Hannah, Lord, I willingly hand over my only son to you.[18] He is yours and of your own do I give You. But just to You. No-one else but You. If You don't have him Lord, send him back. I'm only giving him to You."

I lifted my head and stroked his eyebrows. He was my handsome, strong boy. I kissed him on the hair just above his ear. But as I rose to look at him, Mike's colour returned ever so slightly. Then I saw movement ripple across his face, like the movement of a mirage.

41

It was as if I saw 'a cloud as small as a man's hand on the horizon' in answer to my fervent prayers.[19] I got up, went to the door and looked back. I was sure I could still see the movement on his face.

✶ ✶ ✶

Mike's oldest sister, Akíla, had only just arrived in the Caribbean with the ship *Logos Hope*. After the news was sent to her, we had to fly her home again then help her through the awful process of seeing her brother at the funeral home.

Amazingly, our funeral director, Sam, went to church with Mikey. Mark and I worked with Sam's brother so we were connected in a really personal way. As soon as the autopsy was performed, Sam prepared Mike in the clothes I had provided for him. He then came to our house to talk things through with Akíla.

It was 8:30pm but Sam kindly opened the funeral home for us. Mark and his Mum went in first as a way of breaking the ice for our girls. It was also for Mark, who wanted to see his boy. He hadn't seen Mikey in five days and had missed him so much. My brother Bill, Lorna and I went in next. As I approached the coffin, I saw once again Mikey's colour return and a hint of movement rippled across his face.

The rest of our time there was taken up with Akíla, who was struggling to get through the door. While Mike's younger sister was strong (having been through the process at home) Akíla had never seen a dead body and didn't know what to expect. She wanted to see Mike one last time and she didn't want to go home until she saw him. Yet somehow, she couldn't get further than the threshold. It took Akíla close on half an hour to walk less than three metres towards Mike!

We stayed as long as Akíla needed to stay then eventually left when she was ready to go.

I had a restless night.

I preferred to remember Mike in his own room, on his own pillow, lying under his duvet with his stuffed dog next to him. The image of him in a lace-covered casket, his lips that had so longed to praise God — (those lips I loved to kiss when he was small, and wished I could get near when he was older, though he wouldn't let me) — those lips were sealed closed.

This was utterly grievous! These images weren't something I wanted imprinted on my mind.

I seemed to wrestle with God in fitful sleep until the early hours of the morning. I was trying to re-print over unwanted impressions in my mind. Yet even through all this, I was the first to bring Mikey into the world and the last to see him leave the house — including that horrible, yet necessary process at the funeral home — yet God was still God to me.

At the eye of the storm God gave me 'treasures of darkness stored in secret places'.[20] In the stillness of death, He seemed to show me something that I now believe Jesus may have seen on the face of a young girl in the *Book of Matthew*. A younger girl had died but her Father came to Jesus. He was convinced that if Jesus laid his hand on her, she would live.

When Jesus arrived at the man's home, it was filled with mourners who were weeping loudly. When He saw them He said to them all, "The girl's not dead but asleep."[21]

We have since found a photo of Mike asleep in the front seat of our car. His mouth was slightly ajar. His eyes were ever-so-slightly open.

The photo of Mike asleep on that car journey is the same face we saw on August 1st...

...*Don't cry, he's just asleep* ...

Although the road has since been long, we have experienced some interesting 'God-incidents' where the supernatural seemed to step momentarily into the natural. This was one of those 'God moments'.

In that quiet place at the storm's core, Mike's Maker seemed to show me His compassion. He gave only me this one *breadcrumb:* to be able to see LIFE, even on the face of death, and it has sustained me ever since.

- The Joy You All Once Knew -

There are no words that can dispel
The pain within your heart
No words to give you courage
When your lives are torn apart
No words to ease or comfort
The loss of one so dear
But the love you shared in this life
Will keep him always near

Mike was a lovely handsome boy
Your precious son and brother
He left you loving memories
To share with one another
Just close your eyes and feel again
The joy you all once knew
The happiness he brought your lives
While he was here with you

He'll always live within your hearts
Keep Faith in God alive
To know that you will meet again
Will help you to Survive
For this is God's own promise
To all of us – everyone
We will meet again in heaven
When our race on earth is run

Time will not alter anything
And Mike will n'er grow old
But he will be restored to you
To keep, to Love, to Hold

Forever in the arms of Jesus – August 1st 2009

Poem *The Joy You All Once Knew* written for us by
Mike's Australian Grandmother – Dorothy Moore
01.08.09
(Used with Permission)

8. THE HORN OF GIDEON

It was mid-2003 and I was surprised to hear her voice when I answered the phone. Ruth was a very close friend from our Australian church. Tentatively, she explained what God seemed to be impressing upon her heart. It was something for Mike who was twelve years old at the time.

Ruth had done this once before for Mike's sister. A couple of years earlier, she had given our daughter a 'ring of commitment' from God in response to what she felt was His instructions. Our daughter still wears that ring today. So I felt confident that I could trust Ruth's sincere thoughts.

In this latest phone call, Ruth explained that she'd been reading the story of Gideon[22] in the *Book of Judges* in the Bible. He lived in the Bronze Age before Israel had a king. She felt that Mike was somehow connected to Gideon — that he had what she could only describe as 'a Gideon spirit'.

As cryptic as it was, the message seemed to settle well with us. Gideon seemed to be a quiet person, like Mike. Yet God saw past this timid exterior and called him 'a mighty warrior'. I told Mike about the phone call and told him about the story of Gideon in the Bible.

Over the years, as he was growing up, I encouraged him with the thought that God sees past the exterior to see a brave and mighty warrior inside. At the age where Mike should be reading his Bible for himself, I suggested that he might read stories like the story of Gideon.

In the days immediately after Mikey passed away, I mentioned all this to Mark's Mum. She got out the Bible to read the story.

47

For the first time, I wondered if I'd perhaps been focusing on Gideon himself, and not on the full story.

In the *Book of Judges*, Gideon blew a trumpet and the mighty men of close relation rallied to his side. The concept of a long blast of a Ram's horn isn't something new to the Creator God's story. It was part of the earliest stories at the very start when Israel was entering into their long awaited promises that Father God had told them about.[23] In the last book of the Bible, the Book of Revelation, the trumpet sound will usher in all that Father God has promised for the future of humankind.

At the height of this raging storm, and just like '*manna* from heaven', it seemed to us that God was saying: these men were people who 'wanted to rally' — they had 'the Gideon spirit'. They not only heard the trumpet, but the spirit within them rose up and they immediately responded to the call.

After leaving home rather suddenly in 2007 (to do a six-month stint as a deckhand aboard our ship, *Logos II*), Mike wrote these words on a postcard to his youth group:

"It's just like when Jesus said, 'Follow me!' Immediately, they left their nets and followed Him."[24]

So, as the sun was rising on the morning of August 1st 2009, it was as if the King of Kings and the Lord of Life resounded Gideon's Ram's horn ... and, leaving 'his net' behind (his body and all his possessions), our son went too.

9. THE GIFT OF FLOWERS

Mike didn't have a girlfriend any time during his life. I never really got to find out if there was anyone special who had caught his attention. At one point, I asked him if he liked a girl and, surprised that I should even need to ask, he said, "You would be the first to know if I had a girlfriend. I would bring her home. You would see her here."

He somehow naturally thought that the proper process was to bring the girl home first. This would probably have been even before going the next step in becoming 'officially friends'. This naïve, almost old-fashioned approach to dating made me smile. So when I found a stuffed bear in his cupboard in the days before his last Christmas (and he said it wasn't for his sisters), I was intrigued. A week later, Mike had arranged to meet a girl in town, and the bear went too.

When a convenient moment came, a day or two later, I asked if he liked this mystery girl. He said that he didn't like her 'in that way'. So I gently explained how producing a rather expensive bear for her at Christmas, could be giving her the wrong vibes. This seemed especially so when he told me that she had confided with him over her boyfriend's abuse and her struggle with a bad relationship situation.

However, in the same way that he would treat and feel about his sisters, he simply said, "No. It's okay, Mum. I just wanted to make her feel better."

★ ★ ★

Eight months later our Mike was gone and life had descended into inexplicable turmoil. Then our doorbell rang and the happy face of the flower lady beamed up at me.

"You're getting spoilt today!" she chirped as I received the two beautiful bouquets from her hand. She was only the delivery lady, so I wasn't about to ruin her happy morning by telling her what had just happened to our family, and why people were now sending us flowers.

As I closed the door and turned to take the bouquets to the kitchen, I wondered about this concept of 'being spoilt'. After all, I was getting something really special and I didn't deserve it. I've only once received flowers delivered to the door and that was when we celebrated our 20th wedding anniversary. Our special friends from America sent them.

"How beautiful and fresh," I thought when the scent wafted around me on my way to the kitchen. I couldn't help but wonder who they were from as I set them down on the kitchen bench.

Just as the flowers touched the surface of the kitchen worktop, it was as if Mikey was standing right next to my left elbow in the same way he always had done. In the past, he would hear the doorbell then bound in beside me to ask what it was that had just been delivered.

Quick as a flash, and with no prompting at all, it was as if I heard him say, "There you are Mum, these are to make you feel better."

✷ ✷ ✷

Our pastor and his wife sat on the sofa, another friend close by, and Mark was on a chair that faced the hallway. My voice could be heard drifting in from the front hall where I was on the phone to Mike's older sister. I was explaining to her what I thought that God had just done to our family. What He may be saying and how I thought that we should be responding. Then, in a bid to calm her down in what could surely be the worst storm to hit her life, I repeated the words of a Sunday school song that I had learnt as a little girl:

> *"Trust and obey,*
> *For there's no other way,*
> *To be happy in Jesus,*
> *Than to trust and obey."*

Written by John H. Sammis - 1887

As the conversation came to an end, I suggested that I could pray for her. Hearing this from the lounge room, and without thinking of the guests talking to him, Mark stopped and bowed his head. Without a warning or thought for Mike in his mind to precipitate the following, Mark instantly heard the words, "I'm okay, Dad."

These were the only times in this storm that Mark and I felt a real sense that Father God was giving us messages, as if they were directly from Mike. The Creator first identified Himself as 'compassionate'.[25] Now He gave us 'sweet, honey tasting *manna*' in those two spontaneous moments: to hear, as if in Mike's voice, what God Himself would want to say.

"Thank-you Lord, for your compassion and loving-kindness — even in the darkest hours of this storm."

10. QUIET TIMES

The following are prayers from a diary that I had kept for Mikey. I kept one for each of my children and wrote throughout their childhood about memories, development updates and prayers. The idea was to give them their 'life book' when they grew up but Mike didn't get to see his.

September 1990 — 3½ months before Mike's birth.

To my baby. In honour of health and peace and in dedication to future life and happiness. May the Face of God smile upon you in the innermost parts and bring you to Fullness of Life. Your Mother's love.

26/3/91 — Mike, 2 months old.

I pray that God will stand by His promise to save our whole house. I pray He will protect you against the lies of the devil and bring you safely through to Fullness of LIFE.

06/10/91 — Mike, almost 9 months old.

I love you incredibly and pray continually for God's protection over your life. Each day I want to come closer to Him in order to come closer to you. I want to lift you up right now and ask for God's grace to shine in your life. May He protect you from the evil one and draw you into His Kingdom.

52

Either I have a very weird daily Bible reading book of notes, or else God has a copy of it in heaven! He seems to be using it to speak to me precisely and quite uncannily, at just the right moments. I sometimes wonder if He holds off events or brings events forward, to time them with my *QUIETIMES*[26] book (written by Max E. Anders) that He knows I'll be reading either that day, in the days before, or soon after.

Throughout this book, my second book, and on my website www.kathyknight.org I'll be mentioning my *QUIETIMES* book because of the role it played in this storm-filled journey.

It isn't a magical book. It's just an additional tool for understanding what I'm reading in the Bible. The sub-title is: *A Complete Day-by-Day Guide to Personal Worship and Bible Study.* There's a vast array of these sorts of books on the market. Mine is laid out for 365 days. It gives me a chapter per day from the Bible to read, followed by a simple explanation.

I have included *QUIETIMES* on my website. I invite you to visit www.kathyknight.org and click on the *LookUpBooks-UK* page to find my list of recommended books. But because I've owned and used this book for more than 20 years — I bought it from our ship's bookshop in 1990 — copies may now be hard to come by!

With the help of this modern tool in paper format, our Maker seemed to be using His ancient and epic drama in Bible times to comfort and guide our family in our own life-storm. He did this in the following ways...

The Book of JOB

Our local church here in the UK was systematically going through the Bible, beginning on January 1st 2009. The idea was to read set chapters during the week with explanation notes attached. The Pastor would then speak on Sunday either on one topic covered in the reading plan, or give an overview talk on the whole section spanning that week.

It was now eight months after starting this complex task of covering 39 books and 929 chapters of the Old Testament over 365 days. Of all the books to cover right on this particular weekend, the story of Job landed on Sunday August 2nd. Job is a guy in the Bible who may have lived in the vicinity of modern day Uzbekistan. He wrote about the worst storm to hit anyone's life and it happened to him.

Our church was covering Job's story on the day after we stood shaking from head to foot (just as Job no doubt had done) and saying to each other, "This is God. It has to be God. This doesn't happen. It's too weird *not* to be God."

My *QUIETIMES* book put the *Book of Job* Chapter One on July 22nd and covered God's response to Job on July 23rd. This is what I wrote just nine days before our own storm hit:

"Dear Lord, Job had a lot more to worry about than me. He had everything that he loved and owned taken away from him in a single day. I could say that happened to me 25 years ago when I left behind everything I knew in Australia. Or when we escaped our shipwreck. But Job lost 10 children, then was infected with unthinkable sores. Thank you for the hope in there is in Job story: you'll protect us as far as we can cope with it. Help me not to be cynical, as Job's wife seemed to be."

54

Nine days later, Mark and I stood clutching each other in our bedroom with our youngest daughter, while the medics worked on Mike. My mind immediately visualised Job's shocked face as he rose to his feet with each wave of destruction that hit him and his family on that fateful day. Like Job, I could only say, "God is in control. He did this. He has to be involved. God gives and He takes away."

No-one can take breath away (certainly not in the way it happened to Mike) except the Creator who put that breath there in the first place.[27] At God's command, as Sustainer of the Universe, the sustaining power that brought Mike life had been withdrawn.

We found ourselves that first Sunday morning in church (the only place on earth we wanted to be) opening the Scriptures to feed on the *breadcrumbs* in our out-of-body surreal state. The story of Job was being retold from the front. I let it wash around me, and over me, and through me. Like Job, I was determined not to give up or give in. I wanted to worship my Maker as Job did — as Mike would have wanted me to.

✷ ✷ ✷

The Book of PSALMS — Psalm 90

Three days before Mike left us, my *QUIETIMES* book covered Psalm 90. As my eyes passed over the words: *"The length of our days is seventy years — or eighty, if we have the strength; yet their span is but trouble and sorrow, for they quickly pass, and we fly away"*[28], I could hear the strain of a violin floating across eternity towards me. It pulled at my heart strings and caused a lump in my throat. I leant back on my pillows and tried to recall a time when I heard that music before.

I had assumed that all the Psalms (the songs or poems in the *Book of Psalms* in the Bible) were written around King David's time (the second king of Israel). If they weren't written by David, it didn't matter who wrote them. Who reads the heading at the top anyway? Isn't it the words that count?

Now I realised Moses had penned this one and it was called *The Prayer of Moses*. Just like me, he had a quiet time and wrote down prayers. I wondered if he'd written this one on parchment. I imagined it hanging on a wall of his tent. Perhaps he read it each morning before facing the 'trouble and sorrow' each day that came with leadership. This is the life of the leader and the length (the span of leadership years) is determined by the strength you have to endure them.

But my quiet time that day focused on the absence of trouble and sorrow in my life. So in my diary I wrote:

"Lord, I do thank you today. I thank you for the sun pouring in my window. Thank you for my life. I'm a lucky person. Your mercies endure forever. In your mercy you have heard all of my prayers and I live a life of luxury and peace. Like Mark's grandmother often said, 'I have a lot to be thankful for.' I live a lucky life."

Three days after reading this, our storm hit and as I crawled into bed at the end of that tumultuous day, the day that changed our family forever, I remembered saying:

"What's changed, God? The only thing that's changed is, Mike's not here. It's like we were all splashing about with a beach ball in the swimming pool when Mike got out of the pool. You're still here, God. You're still involved and you're still God. I'll still praise you. For the sake of Mike and his desire to worship you, I *will* praise you."

The Book of PROVERBS — Chapter 1

It was 11:00 p.m. five days after Mike passed away from us when I made my way to bed. I wasn't exactly tired so, for the first time in days, I got out my Bible and *QUIETIMES* book. The book is dated for each day. But for the life of me, I couldn't think what day it was! My Pastor was arriving the next morning from Australia so, I figured it was August 5th.

However, as I turned the pages back, I found myself counting back to the day Mike left. The last turn of the page brought me to August 1st. Then I read the amazing chapter in the Bible that was assigned to that day.

It was as if in a very powerful way, Mike's Maker had left us a message on the day He took our son. It could have been a personal letter written from God to Mike. I saw it in four parts:

The first part, v1-7, explained what a proverb is. It was probably an introduction to the whole book. So when God gets to the heart of what He wanted to say, He started with honouring Mark and me:

"Listen, my son, to your father's instruction and do not forsake your mother's teaching. They are a garland to grace your head and a chain to adorn your neck."[29]

In some cultures, at the time when the *Book of Proverbs* was written, a garland on the head and a chain on the neck was literally *all* that was worn for clothing! These two seem to be the first, basic and essential items.

And so, on this of all days, it was as if Mike's maker placed Mark and me in high esteem through these words. Perhaps this was even like when He entrusted Jesus into the hands of his earthly parents, Joseph and Mary.

But over the years I wondered if I'd prayed enough with Mike or read enough of the Bible to him. I never knew if he'd even pray on his own. How much of the Bible did he know?

Yet here, God seemed to be pouring out His love, firstly to honour us and then to actually incorporate our input into the design of Mike's invisible (therefore probably eternal) attire. So as the tears began to flow, I felt sure that Father God was telling me that we'll see Mike again and that He'll be wearing the garland on his head and the chain around his neck. The gifts that Mark and I gave to him in this life.

As I re-read this passage in Proverbs 1, I was also struck by *what* God was saying. God was clearly calling the reader *His son*. Then everything God asked him to avoid, Mikey had avoided. A whole other *breadcrumb* came from this thought. You can read about it in Chapter 13: *Who Ate the Biscuits?* Suffice to say, God seemed to be giving us a clear message on the day when Mike left Planet Earth. That he had attained all what he had been asked to attain, and that in a sense he'd 'peaked' and left at the best time he could.

As I looked back over Mike's life in the earliest days of this storm, I remembered standing on Jesus' own prayer in the Bible and I prayed it throughout Mike's life:

"My prayer is not that you take them out of the world but that you protect them from the evil one."[30]

Over the years, I came in behind that prayer and I prayed that God would protect him and his sisters from the evil one. But maybe 'protecting Mike from the evil one' in this case *was* to take him out of this world. Whatever the reason, I still believe that God had answered my prayers that I unwittingly prayed for him, even before he was born. He has led Mike safely into the 'fullness of LIFE'.

58

There was yet one more thing that was very powerful about this reading that fell directly on the day that Mike left this life. I saw it in v20–33 and it made me think of the parting of some heroic figure. It was as if one of the great leaders in the Bible was dying and they were leaving 'one last powerful speech' for those who they were leaving behind.

Laying back on my pillows alone in my room as I thought of all these things, I could see Wisdom personified and standing in the main street of our town. At the head of the noisy streets she cries out. At the entrance of the gates in the city she recites her ancient words:

"How long, O naive ones, will you love being simple-minded? And scoffers delight themselves in scoffing … Because I called and you refused … and no one paid attention but neglected all my counsel … When your dread comes like a storm and your calamity comes like a whirlwind …

Then they will call on me, but I will not answer; They will seek me diligently but they will not find me … But he who listens to me shall live securely, And will be at ease from the dread of evil."

In my imagination, I could see Wisdom's messenger standing in the main shopping center outside Mike's work. I quietly wondered how Mike's story and the message of God's existence and involvement in modern life, could be used openly to impact the place where Mikey lived and died.

✶ ✶ ✶

A year passed by from the night that I sat contemplating what could have happened to Mike and why. When it came around to August 1st 2010, and I was turning the pages my *QUIETIMES* book to that momentous day, another interesting *breadcrumb* was found. Something that I hadn't noticed in the 20 years of using this book.

The author, Max E. Anders, used further Bible verses each day to help the reader pray, tell God about the things they're sorry for, and to praise or thank God. These extra Bible passages are then repeated in a pattern throughout the year. It's a sort of tool to remind the reader of key truths. If repeated regularly enough, in time these become familiar.

The verse that reads: *"This is the day which the Lord has made; Let us rejoice and be glad in it"*[81], is repeated twelve times in my *QUIETIMES* book. It's positioned on the 5th day of every month ... except one. For some reason only known to the original author, the pattern changed for August. Differing from all the other months, the author chose instead to place this verse and these words on the page for August 1st!

I see this as a most peculiar 'coincidence' in a book that I bought more than 20 years before that most devastating August 1st — the probability of which someone else could work out, if they should bother to take the time!

Or was it something other than mere coincidence?

Was it some important communication perhaps, and known only to the Creator God? Was it a *breadcrumb* that He left there especially for me in my hour of extreme need? On the very day I needed it, He was telling me that He has made *this day too*. If I choose to trust Him, I *can* 'rejoice and be glad' in that day too.

✶ ✶ ✶

60

The Book of LAMENTATIONS — Chapter 3

There are 66 books in the Bible and 1189 chapters. But there are only 365 chapters that had the possibility of being picked to feature in my *QUIETIMES* book. There are 365 days in a year but only 52 weeks to cover the 66 books — if my *QUIETIMES* book is to give a good overview for anyone seeking to have a daily Bible reading, as the subtitle denotes.

There is only one book in the Bible where Father God's extended family expressed real 'weeping and gnashing of teeth'. My *QUIETIMES* book gave only one chapter for this heart-wrenching book of poetic laments in the whole year. The author of *QUIETIMES* chose Lamentations 3 for August 12th — the date that the funeral director gave for Mike's funeral.

In a book that I bought 20 years before our most grievous moment, this was what the God of Creation knew I'd be reading on the day that we buried our lovely son:

"He [God] pierced my heart with arrows from His quiver ...

Yet this I call to mind and therefore I have hope: Because of the LORD's great love we are not consumed, for His compassions never fail ...I say to myself, 'The LORD is my portion; therefore I will wait for Him.' ...

It is good for a man to bear the yoke while he is young ...

Though [God] brings grief, He will show compassion, so great is His unfailing love...

For He does not willingly bring affliction or grief to the children of men...

Who can speak and have it happen if the Lord has not decreed it? Is it not from the mouth of the Most High that both calamities and good things come?"[32]

On the day that we had committed our lovely boy to the ground, I couldn't help but believe that the Creator God was telling us that He knew how we felt. Through this reading, it seemed to me that:

- God took ownership for our grief [v13, 37 and 38], but
- He did not willingly bring this affliction on us [v33].
- It was even good for Mike to leave early — while he was young [v27].
- Though this is hard to bear, God has compassion [v32].

Now, in the spirit of Moses (who wrote Psalm 90), Job (who lost everything he had), King Solomon (who wrote the Proverbs) and Jeremiah (who wrote the laments) — and because of the Lord's great love and His compassions that never fail [v22] — we will say to ourselves, "The Lord is our portion; therefore we will wait for Him." [v24].

In all that I've seen and heard over those destabilising days before and after Mike's passing and in the long journey since, I've come to see once again that Jesus was right:

"...Man does not live by bread alone, but by every word that proceeds from the mouth of God."[83]

Through all these extraordinary coincidences that continued to rain down during the month of August 2009, we came to see and hear our Maker's supernatural communication with us. It led our family to believe beyond reasonable doubt that the Creator God (who carefully and quite miraculously preserved His Word for us to read today) not only exists, but is also concerned. He fed us with 'manna from heaven' — His *Breadcrumbs in this Storm*.

11. PRAISE YOU IN THIS STORM

It was around 4 a.m. while aboard the newest OMSI ship in the Caribbean, when Mike's older sister, Akíla, was woken to receive the news of her brother's death.

Our friends, Peter and Win, were the first people Mark had phoned after he found our Michael, and their response was immediate. Peter was making most of the necessary phone calls for us from our house that morning. So he phoned the Ship's Director while they were berthed in St Vincent in the Caribbean. After receiving that call, his wife Anne, and their daughter went looking for Akíla.

Because our daughter is hearing impaired, once she takes out her hearing aid she doesn't hear the usual sounds that the rest of us hear. The sorts of sounds that would often keep the rest of us in shallower levels of sleep. So Akíla wouldn't have heard footsteps or whispering in the alleyway outside her cabin; a door opening; a cabin mate stirring and turning over in bed. Because of this, Akíla sleeps deeply. That night, she'd also gone to bed very late. So this unscheduled awakening was particularly disorientating for her.

Since two other girls also shared that cabin, Anne simply asked Akíla to get dressed and to follow her and her daughter. But by the time she entered the cabin of our Ship's Director and saw that their bed was made up and stowed away for the day, Akíla's mind was spinning.

Stepping through the door she was certain that something had happened to her Dad, or even her adventurous younger sister.

Nothing could have prepared her for the shocking news that her healthy, strong and active eighteen-year-old brother was gone. He left us in his sleep and for no reason at all!

Naturally, Akíla burst out with a few 'choice words' in her bewildered disbelief!

Once she was settled enough to return to her own cabin, Akíla walked in on her two confused cabin mates and simply said, "Well, my brother just died!" She then headed straight to the communal shower room down the alleyway where she dissolved into uncontrollable wailing. All the girls in her accommodation section were in a state of total shock! They avoided using that shower room just to give her space.

For several minutes Akíla stood under the running water and sobbed until there were no more tears left to weep. This was all she could muster. The ship's nurse, and a close friend of ours, was quietly waiting when she surfaced — to comfort her, and to no doubt offer her medication for her pounding head!

When the news broke in the early morning meeting for the ship's crew and staff, the onboard worship team led the ship's community with the song *Praise You in This Storm* by the Gospel music group *Casting Crowns*. Upon returning home to the UK, Akíla mentioned the song to us and we wondered if Mike had it in his music collection. Over the next days we scanned Mike's room for his MP3 player.

At the time, I had presumed that this was to find this song.

Mike had been given an iPod for his eighteenth birthday. When his younger sister turned this on for the first time, the song highlighted was *Saviour King* from Hillsong Australia. We felt sure that this was the last song that Michael had listened to on his iPod.

64

During the afternoon before he left us, Mark wanted Michael to help him cut back a vine at the back of our house. He found Michael in his room playing his guitar along to *Saviour King*. It was the last song that he listened to on his iPod and the last song that he played on his guitar. We used this song in Mike's funeral service — his 'Celebration of Praise' Thanksgiving service.

But now we were looking for Mike's MP3 player. The songs he'd loaded to it were songs that caught his interest from the ages of 15 to 17. But neither Mark nor I were keen on moving anything around in Mike's room to find it. It was his younger sister who eventually found it — producing it like the finding of lost treasure! Mark put the MP3 player next to his bed and planned to listen through it when he had time.

It was by then Friday night — the seventh night without Mike. Akíla, Mark and my brother from Australia were out by the outdoor fire in the garden. I was heading to bed when Mark came to check on me.

As he was leaving the room he said, "I just wanted to let you know that tomorrow is Saturday. It'll be one week since last Saturday morning, when we found Mike. You may need to be ready. It might be hard. Are you okay with that?"

"Oh," I said, "I'm so spaced out. I wouldn't have a clue what day of the week it is. I can't time milestones like that. I'm fine."

But I hadn't been fine on any of the nights! I would wake and wonder what was happening in Mike's room in the early hours of that final Saturday morning. Every night I hated walking past Mike's bedroom door. I didn't want the door closed. But I also didn't want it wide open like a yawning black hole. As irrational as it sounds, I felt most comfortable with it partially opened.

I slept for three hours but I was wide awake at 2 a.m. on that first Saturday morning without Mike. My stirring must have alerted Mark to me being awake, as he already was. So by 3 a.m. we sat up and began talking and praying and grappling and discussing as we had done every waking hour that week. Just before dawn I suggested making tea and toast.

When I returned to our room, Mark was in tears. He'd just had what he could only describe as a 'God-moment'! When I left the room he reached for Mike's MP3 player, went click, click, click ... and the first song was the very song Akíla had told us about:

Praise You in This Storm
- Casting Crowns -

*I was sure by now, God you would have reached down
And wiped our tears away, Stepped in and saved the day
But once again, I say "Amen", and it's still raining
As the thunder rolls
I barely hear You whisper through the rain: "I'm with you"
And as Your mercy falls
I raise my hands and praise the God
who gives and takes away*

*I'll praise You in this storm, And I will lift my hands
For You are who You are, No matter where I am
Every tear I've cried, You hold in Your hands
You never left my side, And though my heart is torn
I will praise You in this storm*

*I remember when I stumbled in the wind
You heard my cry to You, You raised me up again
My strength is almost gone, How can I carry on,
If I can't find You
And as the thunder rolls...*

66

I lift my eyes unto the hills, Where does my help come from?
My help comes from the Lord,
The Maker of Heaven and Earth

And I'll praise You in this storm…

Extract taken from the song 'Praise You in This Storm' by Mark Hall and Bernie Herms © 2005 Song Solutions*
(See Copyright Page for full Acknowledgement)

As we wept through the extraordinarily fitting words in this amazing song, we wondered who this boy was! What fifteen to seventeen-year-old boy would load his MP3 with such a powerful song? Mike wanted to become a worship leader and now he was leading *us* into worship in the greatest storm of our lives.

More than this though, our minds were blown away by our Perfect God's perfect timing. Perhaps even to the very moment where Michael's 'day and hour' was released[34] by The Father in Heaven, just seven days before.

Over the coming days that song became a kind of theme song. It led us into profound worship in unfathomable grief. On the morning of August 12th, while dressing for Mikey's funeral, I listened to it at high volume. Over and over again I replayed it while trying to do my hair through blinding tears.

In the darkness of our room before the dawn on that first Saturday morning without our lovely boy, only God Himself could have planned and timed this poignant 'find' right down to the moment so precisely. It was a *breadcrumb* left behind by our beloved son. In time, it would feed and sustain us on this rock-strewn road of grief and praise. It was yet another moment to strengthen us as we began our long journey back to enduring faith in the God who Mike still worships.

12. THE FUNERAL DRESS

I was woken with the phone ringing one Friday morning in early June 2009. My Australian church Pastor was firm, "Kath, I've thought about it," she said, "how would you feel about coming home?"

The church's Missions Coordinator, and a very kind friend to us, was the second to pass away in a matter of weeks. So the faith of the Believers there had taken a real beating. My mind raced onto a looming Tax exam I'd prepared for. Then, the week after that, there was the grand finale prepared in London that would launch our largest ship. We'd been waiting and preparing eight years for that event!

But all of this took a back seat in that one moment. I phoned Mark (who was aboard our ship in Wales at the time) to begin arrangements for returning home. The next hours were spent on the Internet getting the next available flight to Australia. By Saturday afternoon I was standing in a shop trying on a dress to wear for Jean's funeral.

Mark arrived home to be with our kids, and after showing him the dress (and looking in this mirror and that mirror), I decided I would return it to the shop. I don't buy clothes that often, and this dress just didn't seem to fit with this funeral. I gave Mark my credit card and the receipt, and asked him to return the outfit after I left.

In the early days of the following month, Mark and I were in the car again, on our way home from the airport. As usual, he was filling me in on all the comings and goings of the past four weeks while I was away. He then happened to say that the shop wouldn't take the funeral dress back.

I immediately figured I'd keep it for some other occasion. It was the sort of dress that would be right for one of our Ship Project Donor events. I could see myself wearing it while drinking a cup of tea at a finger-food buffet.

But then Mark clarified: "They gave me a credit note instead. They also want you to use it in the next six months."

That was a real disappointment. I never shop at that store. Unfortunately, the dress was a little bit too expensive to waste on a mistake! After apologising to Mark, I hoped that I'd find something in that shop in a few weeks.

By the end of the first week back in the UK, and by then five weeks since I first bought the dress, we decided to visit that shop again.

When I went in, I asked about the outfit I'd originally bought. It seemed to be the only thing I liked in that shop! The shop assistant found that one was left. I then handed her the receipt and explained to her that I'd bought different sizes of each of the three pieces that made up the outfit. She would have to check what I originally bought, to see if those sizes were the same as the dress that hung on the rack. Each piece was the size that I wanted!

She then noticed that the tags were worn and said, "You know, I think this is the same outfit that you returned." I couldn't believe it! This doesn't happen. "The same dress and five weeks later," I marvelled, as I hung it in my wardrobe.

✶ ✶ ✶

As I stood in front of my wardrobe spaced out and numb, from the tornado that had just hit our home, I mindlessly wondered what I would put on just to eat breakfast!

When your only son passes away suddenly and unexpectedly, why would you contemplate getting out of bed at all — ever! Had I not had my brother and sister-in-law downstairs; Mark's Mum about to arrive for breakfast from where we'd housed her down the street; or my Pastor, her husband and my two sisters who had all flown in from Australia to be with us (and were due to walk over mid-morning from their accommodation), I would simply walk around in a dressing gown. I could ride out the day under a blanket on the sofa — or simply stay in bed!

As my wrung-out brain scanned the clothes hanging in my wardrobe, my eyes alighted on a blue dry cleaner's bag. I knew exactly what was inside.

Going immediately down stairs with the prized bag, I recounted my story to the others. Two months after purchasing a funeral dress (and with the tags still on it), what was unsuitable for the one funeral, was perfect for my son. He had just completed basic training on Planet Earth; received his graduation certificate from his youth group; and possessed a letter of full recommendation from our ship's captain. He was now to have his 'passing out ceremony'.

When funerals can often be somber with everyone wearing black, the topic of 'what to wear' was on everyone's mind. We never expected to be saying goodbye to Mike so what would be the overall feel or message that Mike would want? What do we communicate to the guests?

All of us were thinking of what to wear and all, in our own way, wanted to honour Mike for our own reasons.

Mark was set on wearing his Hawaiian shirt. He had visited Mike on the ship in the Caribbean and had taken him to the beach for a boy's day out. When Mark returned home he chose for his FaceBook profile picture a certain photo from that day with Mike. In it the two boys, both father and son, were beaming at the camera. Mike had grubby knees from his deck work and Mark was wearing his Hawaiian shirt.

Some time had passed and we happened to go on Mike's FaceBook page, only to find that he had chosen the same photo for his own profile picture. So the Hawaiian shirt had to take central place in Mark's heart and mind on the day he would be forced to walk away from his son.

Mike's sisters were dressed in beautiful dresses that were bought for the occasion. They were determined to dress as beautifully as they could for their brother. They would now miss out on his wedding, and all the other special events, so they planned together to dress up for him for this, his last event on earth.

In my mind I could see now that my dress would be exactly the sort of dress that a parent would wear on the decks of a huge aircraft carrier in Pearl Harbor. We would be drinking cups of tea at a finger-food buffet while attending our son's 'passing out ceremony'. Mike was passing from basic training on earth, and moving into His Majesty's Royal Service in Eternity.

My dress was bought for a funeral but returned to the shop. It was left for five weeks then re-bought again. This funeral outfit, that had hung untouched in my wardrobe with the price tags still on it, had taken a long journey before finding its original and rightful purpose. Though I had no idea of any of this when I stood trying it on in the store's changing room two months earlier, it was a use that Father God no doubt knew of from that very first day.

As I returned the dry cleaning bag to my wardrobe to await that momentous day, in three days' time, I couldn't help but think that this was only one of the many coincidences.

Taking all these moments as a collective whole though, it seems more likely that they were never coincidental in the first place. Instead, they showed us the controlling hand of the *God who Knows All Things*. He seemed to organise even the smallest of details as He arranged for us to receive His *Breadcrumbs in this Storm*.

13. WHO ATE THE BISCUITS?

The danger in losing one of your prized possessions is that you could end up painting them in a different light than what was, in fact, reality. We tend to deify those we love most when we no longer have them left to love.

During the morning on which our lovely son died, I was in the shower after the ambulance and police left our house. My mind wandered onto the words from the *Book of Hebrews*:

"...*man is destined to die once, after this comes judgment*..."[85]

From Scripture I could see that there is a judgement day with a judge. The Bible calls it the "Day of the Lord". If that's the case, then there must be an accuser. But who are the witnesses? Is there a jury? If I had a chance to testify at the Michael's judgement, I would say, "This boy did nothing wrong."

I had to catch myself because only Jesus was found to be without sin. No accusation was found that could be brought against Him at His crucifixion. The written charge in Roman Law against Him, and the reason why He was sentenced to death, read not what He had *done* wrong, but only *who He was*.[36] So then, if only Jesus could be found without a charge that could be brought against Him when He was judged, what *was* wrong with our Mikey?

Mike had one fault that I knew of: he seemed to have a problem lying over who ate the biscuits. Looking back, it was probably my fault for asking, "Who ate *all* the biscuits?" The packet was empty. But Mike could rightly say, "It wasn't me" if he hadn't eaten *all* the biscuits. That is to say: he only ate *most* of them, or *the last* of them!

I remember standing outside his room a few years before, when I told Mark, "I think Mike has a problem with lying." I'm not sure what I expected Mark to do about it. It was infuriating finding wrappers in Mike's bin after he said it wasn't him!

I stopped typing this story at this point in order to make myself a cup of tea. I opened the snack cupboard to find the plastic biscuit barrel bearing the words, "Lunch Box Only!" I wish now for that biscuit barrel to be found empty — just for one last time. I'd give all the biscuits in the world to have Mikey home for one more day. If not to eat them all.

… I threw the nasty biscuit barrel away …

★ ★ ★

Within days of Mikey dying, two of my sisters kindly travelled to the UK just to 'be there' for me. As soon as they arrived at our house, Mike's youngest sister appeared from her room. Then, in a baby voice mimicking a child of about five years, one of my sisters said, "Who ate the last biscuit?"

Apparently, when we were visiting her house in Australia one year, our youngest daughter 'became a policeman' after finding that someone had taken the last biscuit on the plate.

Like the Spanish Inquisition, our little girl had gone about the house and out into the garden, interrogating all the children in a bid to track down the perpetrator of the crime: the person who so rudely ate the last biscuit!

All their childhood, I had a real problem with lies from my kids. I didn't mind if one of my kids ate the biscuits. I just wanted to know *who* ate them so that I could tell them *not* to.

74

Eating biscuits would spoil their dinner for example. However, it seemed that 'all of hell broke loose' when they'd lie about it! It would then erupt into pure volcanic activity if I found the wrappers in someone's waste paper basket — namely the one in Mike's bedroom!

It was close to dinner time on Friday July 31st 2009 when Mark and Mikey had finished cutting back the climber on the rear wall of the house. Mark, who has a nut allergy and ordinarily doesn't eat chocolate, had bought himself a packet of Cadbury's chocolate finger biscuits earlier in the week. This was to be his treat while sipping his coffee in a break from painting our lounge room. Before putting the biscuits in the cupboard, he gave some to the kids, two he gave to me, and then he said, "Okay, these are mine now. No-one eat them."

Since we were late preparing dinner that night, Mark decided to have a coffee with one of his prized biscuits, but the cupboard was bare! I was painting something in the kitchen when Mark called out, "Okay, who ate my biscuits?"

Instantly, Mike appeared from the lounge room and said, "I ate the last four."

We were shocked! All we could do was stand there praising him for his honesty. No-one knows what happened to that biscuit conversation, nor whether or not Mark got his cup of coffee after that! The idea of Mike confessing so freely, without being questioned a second time, was enough to blow all of us away! … That was the last direct conversation we had with Mike before he died.

★ ★ ★

As I stood in the bathroom the next morning, mulling over the concept of judgement (and if I were to be called forward as a witness on Mike's life before the Judge of the World), I would say, "This boy was without sin. He did nothing wrong to us and we're the closest ones to him. Even that one vice, that 'thorn in the flesh' that he *did* seem to have, was mastered on his last day on earth."

The Bible says that God's Holy Spirit is living and active inside all Believers. His job is to "sanctify" us. That means to clean, train, and change us for all our lives. If so, could it be that God waited for that last sin to be mastered, before He deemed Mikey ready to be taken? It was as if God was saying, "I can change even quirky little faults that Mike was blamed for."

Even if it was only just another strange coincidence, we took that amazing event less than 12 hours before he died as yet another *breadcrumb* sent directly from God as we marvelled over His goodness in the events of Mike's final hours on earth.

14. SAVED THROUGH FAITH

Since Mike was a quiet boy, my biggest worry was: where he stood with God? Yes, he spent all of his spare time playing his guitar to Gospel music, but was that a good enough indication that he was acceptable?

Mike had been 'dedicated' (prayed for) as a baby but he hadn't been publicly baptised. After gentle encouragement about adult baptism at twelve years old (that his sister called 'scaring him into it'), I backed off. I simply prayed that God's Holy Spirit would encourage him to go that next step. If it was that important to God, surely *He* needed to prompt Mike and get him to *want* to be baptised.

Nine days before Mike left us, I read in the *Book of Job* how Job had offered sacrifices for his children after each of their parties, just in case they *'sinned and cursed God in their hearts'*.[37] I wondered what sacrifice I could make for my kids. Praying for your kids is one important thing but what about commitment and baptism from their side?

With Mike's Uncle soon to arrive from Australia, I pictured him and Mark baptising Mike. I thought of prompting Mike with the topic of baptism once more. I didn't get the chance. None of us could have guessed that my brother and Mark's role together was not to lower him into the waters of baptism but was instead to lower Mikey into the ground.

What was really weird was that Mike's church had a baptism service planned for the week *after* Mike left! So as soon as the police left the house that momentous morning, I quietly asked Mike's Pastor about baptism. I wanted to know what Mike's church understood from Jesus' words:

"*Truly, truly, I tell you, no one can enter God's Kingdom unless they are born of water and the Holy Spirit.*"[38]

Father God must have known this was playing on my mind and to quieten my fears, He not only gave us the *breadcrumb* in the last chapter (the mastering of Mike's quirky little fault on his last day here), but He also gave us the following:

August 1st — Proverbs 1

"*My son, if sinners entice you, don't give in to them. If they say, 'Come with us ... throw in your lot with us ...' — don't go along with them, don't set foot on their paths ... they waylay only themselves! Such is the end of all who go after ill-gotten gain; it takes away the lives of those who get it.*"[39]

This passage came from Proverbs 1 and was set in my daily *QUIETIMES* book for the morning when God took our lovely boy. With it, Mike's Creator God seemed to be telling me that *His* son, Michael, did everything that was asked of him. He stayed away from trouble and kept his life clean. By showing me this passage at that crucial moment, Michael's God seemed to be confirming that Mike was *God's* son, not mine. And that He was a pleasing son: a 'good and faithful servant'.[40]

On the day after Mikey left us, we sat in church listening to the Bible story of Job's catastrophic day. Then, a mobile phone text message came through from a very close friend. It was these words from the *Book of Psalms*:

August 2nd — Psalm 24

"*Who can go up on the hill of the Lord? Who can stand in God's holy place? He who has clean hands and a pure heart ... He will receive vindication from the God of Salvation.*"[41]

By this, Mike's Maker seemed to be confirming that Mike had *clean hands* and as such, was able to *ascend the hill of the Lord* and *stand in His holy place*. That Mike will be saved on the Day of Judgment because he will receive *vindication from God his Saviour*.

As I sat reading this passage, I couldn't help but notice that next to it in the Bible is Psalm 23. It fell to me, at Dad's funeral 10 years before, to read Psalm 23.

Looking down at the open pages in my Bible after losing my lovely boy, it was as if my father and my son now lay side by side in the pages of the Scripture. We included Psalm 24 as the Bible Reading in Mikey's 'Celebration of Praise' — the memorial service on the day that we buried our son.

15. PENTECOST IN 50 DAYS

I remember the warmth of my brother's arm around me as I sat on the sofa clutching my stomach as if in deep pain. I was weeping for my treasured son. The son that I loved. My only son in whom I was well pleased.

With my eyes closed, it was easy to be transported back in time to another day when another mother sat bent over, clutching *her* stomach and weeping until there was no energy left in any cell of her body.

In my mind's eye I could see three crosses ahead and at some distance from me. Several metres from me, and a little to the right, was a pile of women. Like a pile of rag dolls they'd cried out all their tears. They were now lying in a heap together not caring whose feet they were sitting on, or who was sitting on them. The standing group had simply imploded onto each other. They lay whimpering softly, as the clouds began to gather and darkness began to fall.

With this vision set before me, my focus shifted from Mike to those crosses. I had never wept over the Cross of Christ like I wept that day — just three days after I lost my own son. I could only thank God that I didn't have to see Mike's flesh torn from his body. I didn't have to see his bloodstained face resting lifeless on his chest as he hung so mercilessly from a cruel cross.

But what caught my attention at that moment was another pile of bodies. This was about the same distance from me as the pile of weeping women, but slightly to my left. As I looked I could see that it was a pile of dead angels — only they weren't dead at all!

Like the pile of women (and having being commissioned *not* to intervene), they too had cried out all their tears. They too lay motionless in grief. None of them were able to pull their strength together enough even to move.

I felt God the Father saying: "Now you know how I feel and, I know how you feel." I could only thank God that none of this happened to my only son — my lovely Mikey.

✶ ✶ ✶

On the third day after Mike died, I rose up before daylight — just as the women in the Bible had done.[42] I didn't do it deliberately. I was awake from 3:30 a.m. that Monday. I was thinking of Mary, the mother of Jesus, going to embalm her son's body. Soon it would be time for me to prepare Mike's clothes for his burial. By 4:30 a.m. I got up so as not to disturb Mark, who was snoring at the time. (How I loved the sound of that snore. It was the first time in our marriage I welcomed it!)

In the summer here, surrounded by low horizons that border Scotland, we have long sunrises. The sun seems to skim the horizon for an hour before it breaks over the hills. I sat in our conservatory until after 6:00 a.m. I was watching the clouds change to a beautiful rose red before our household had begun to stir.

I prayed that God would perform 'a jail break' at dawn as He had done for His own son. The door to a morgue is far easier to open than rolling back a large stone (on that first Easter morning) when Jesus' tomb was staked out with a guard of ruthless Roman soldiers! God also sent an earthquake to opened the doors to a jailhouse and break the chains for Paul and Silas, two of Jesus' followers in the Bible.[43]

If an earthquake had struck our town at that moment, I would have been the first in the car heading for the hospital mortuary! When the autopsy was then delayed another two days, I prayed again for Mike's return. Somewhere deep inside though, I was also prepared to let God keep him.

My theological studies showed me several types of Christ in the Old Testament, including the big one on Mount Moriah when Abraham almost lost Isaac, the only son he had left. People who study scripture don't seem to hesitate in saying that this person was like Jesus, or that one's experience was like Jesus'. These stories pointed to something beyond the person and their actual circumstances or life events. These belonged to a bigger picture that would be revealed in time.

In our Summer Newsletter, sent out just days before Mikey passed away, I wrote about the death of our close friend whose time on earth seemed far too short:

"One thing that seems to happen in scripture is 'the seasons in time'. God times things with precise detail. Joseph went into the service of Pharaoh King of Egypt when he was 30. Saul and David were both 30 when they became King of Israel and Jesus Lordship was made visible at 30."

Moses, Saul, David and Solomon all served Israel for 40 years. The Southern Kingdom of Judah was exiled for 70 years. Human life is 'three score and ten' — 70 years and in AD70 (one life span from Jesus birth) the last temple was destroyed. Even the boy Samuel *"grew in stature and in favour with God and man"*.[44] He was the only other person in the Bible who was attributed those words outside of Jesus.

But what about the future? Are we allowed to have a 'type' of Christ now?

Followers of Jesus are taught to be 'Christ-like' in all that we do. As teenagers, our kids wore a wrist band with WWJD on it — *What Would Jesus Do?* This was to help them think twice about choosing and behaving in a way that *wasn't* like Him. And what about life events? Are our own experiences or events allowed to be like His?

As I watched the crimson glow of sunrise three days after our only son died, and thinking of all these things before anyone else stirred, I knew these were all odd questions. Nonetheless, I followed the analogy of the events of Easter, and God losing His only son. Jesus died at the Jewish festival of Passover and, just as the Prophet Joel foretold centuries before, the Holy Spirit came in power on his followers fifty days later — at Pentecost.

Thinking on this, I began comparing it against our own experience as it was unfolding before us. It intrigued me enough to look forward in my *QUIETIMES* book to work out when Day 50 would be. I didn't have a calendar handy so, using my *QUIETIMES* book, I counted the days manually.

With a broad smile of irony, I turned the last page to Day 50 and came face-to-face with yet another so-called coincidence. It was September 19th, the day that Mike had been planning for and working towards for more than a year. He had been working at McDonalds in order to save all his wages towards this day marked out in his mind, and on our kitchen calendar. It was the very day that Mike was due to start his worship training at a music school in Coventry.

The "manna" found in the desert was only for the Children of Israel, and even some of them complained about it. The reading in my *QUIETIMES* book for September 19th was a reading that said: "… *I'm not ashamed of the gospel* …"[45] This was true of Mike's FaceBook and Bebo websites where he called himself *Guitarist for Christ*.[46]

We had the words, *I'm not ashamed* ... put onto Mike's Celebration of Praise service sheet (printed program). We also played the song, *I'm Not Ashamed* by Hillsong Australia, at his memorial service.

The Creator God (who created time in the first place when He set Planet Earth spinning then rotating around our sun), seemed to give this *breadcrumb* especially to me — a piece of well-timed trivia: 50 days to September 19th.

It was another *breadcrumb* that seemed to feed us and sustain us at the outset of what was to become an epic journey of survival. God knew I'd be interested in the trivia embedded within these inexplicable coincidences. They seemed to point unquestionably toward Father God's perfect timing. Mike's Maker had control over every detail of Mike's life, death and resurrection into Eternal LIFE.

16. THE PERFECT NUMBER

The event of a death and subsequent burial of a loved one is one of the worst events anyone has to go through in this life. Not only are you in shock, but you have to endure absurd dialogue over what songs to sing at the funeral service! Mike's sudden and unexpected departure led to an inquest. This at least gave us extra days before the funeral service had to be finalised. How is it possible for anyone to think clearly at a time like this?

One horrible discussion we had was whether or not we were to bury or cremate our lovely boy. We were clearly unprepared! There was never a time at any point in our marriage when we had to debate each other's views on this emotive topic. The funeral director was clearly gifted on how to approach this dreadful situation. He was very kind in his approach and manner. But this subject had more unexpected baggage attached to it than any of us realised.

In the 25 years since leaving Australia, my June 2009 trip back home (just six weeks before Mikey died) was the closest I'd ever come to seeing 'light at the end of the tunnel'. It seemed that God may be finally leading us home to Australia. At nineteen, I'd committed to following my Maker anywhere that He led me. I just forgot to mention for how long!

After getting time in Australia with a significant person in our lives, I came back to tell Mark about a job offer there. Oddly enough, though, I'd also be the first to be worried about the upheaval of leaving the UK. I would only want to return home to Australia if we *all* knew it was the right move. If we knew that God was leading our whole family in this way, to begin a new chapter in our family story there.

However, my life-dream had just exploded in my face in one devastating event. How on earth could I leave now? How could I go to the other side of the planet and leave my lovely boy behind?

We went through a tearful hour until I came to terms with all the options. Both of us erred on the side of burial, but I wanted to be able to take Mike with us when we finally moved to Australia. By the end of it, I had to resign myself to the concept of the missionaries of old who went to places like China and Africa, burying their kids along the way. It seemed to me that God was asking me to do this now.

By the time he was two, Mike had been to 21 countries. The first two years of his life were lived on a ship with 'no ground to call home'. We moved to the UK just before Mike's second birthday. He went to school here, joined the local climbing club here, worked here, and enjoyed a church family and youth group here. It was his home town in every way and he knew it well. Now it seemed fitting for him to be buried here.

This was a moment of sudden truth as I came to terms with a possible future flight home. If that day comes, I'll look through an aeroplane window to see the green fields of the Scottish Borderlands disappear from under my feet. Then, what should be a very happy event in the life of our family, will instead be an event bathed in tears as I leave behind my beloved son. But the *breadcrumbs* continued to fall. God sent us special *'manna* from heaven', to feed us and to tell us *He knows*. It seemed that God wanted to soothe us by giving us "*... oil of joy instead of mourning, and a garment of praise instead of a spirit of despair ...*"[47]

It was three weeks after Mike died. The funeral was over. All the guests were gone, and we were about to leave on a recovery break away with our two girls.

86

Mark gathered up the official papers to be put away until our return. He stopped to look at the coroner's letter. While he was looking at that paper, I had Mike's temporary death certificate in my hand. Then I noticed the reference number.

This coroner deals with a significantly wide area across the north of our county, which is the largest in England. The reference number used is a computer generated number: the next available number. The numbering code is then finished with the year i.e. xxxx–2009. This means that the numbers would start again at 0001 in the new year. It would relate to the number of deaths across the north of the county and referred to that coroner's office for further investigation. Mike's case was to receive the next available number.

Of all possible reference numbers given to Mike's temporary death certificate between 0 and 9999 for the year 2009, Mike's departure was timed precisely to occur; to be referred to this particular coroner, and to be given the next number available on his computer. The number on Mike's temporary death certificate was 777. The full number was 0777–2009.

Throughout the Bible, God often used the number seven. It's not a magic number, but it is a special cyclical number.

At the start of God's story in the Bible there's the seventh day, when God rested from His work of creation. He called the day a 'Sabbath day of rest' that many people still enjoy today. In the last book of the Bible, the *Book of Revelation*, seven is mentioned 54 times. The book opens with a vision of the One who holds the seven stars (representing the seven Spirits of God) in His right hand and walks among the seven golden lamp stands.

On a practical level throughout the history of God's family, the seventh year was when the ground was to be given rest.

On the seventh year slaves were to be set free. Every seventh seven — every 49th year — an additional year of release was added to the seven. This was the 50th year, the 'Year of Jubilee'. A year of jubilation ushered in by a trumpet-blast of liberty for the land, slaves and indentured servants.

After being asked how many times we should forgive someone, Jesus answered, "*I tell you, not seven times, but seventy-seven times.*"[48] Now, Eternal life is based purely and simply on forgiveness. So in this same way, God has shown His capacity to forgive humans of what's happened in past years. He sets us free from our slavery to "sin" — free from indentured servitude to guilt. With a trumpet blast we'll be ushered into His Kingdom with great jubilation![49]

Looking now at the documents in my hand, I felt sure that God had stamped Mikey's death papers three times with His perfect number — seven hundred and seventy-seven. It was a *breadcrumb* sent just for me to find, and to smile at the irony of it, in what would normally be a dark and stormy hour filled only with despair.

17. I AM FREE

In June 2009, our close friends, Todd and Karen (who've walked with us through the deepest places in our life and marriage) had arranged for a one-week holiday for their family. They planned it at a beach apartment on the east coast of America and it was set to begin on August 22nd.

But two things were strange about this.

Firstly, they rarely take a seven-day holiday, and certainly not to a self-catering apartment. They normally take long weekends due to their busy work load. In addition, the apartment had eight beds but there were only three of them!

They began to invite friends to join them, but each declined for varying reasons. By the end of July, Todd and Karen began to wonder if God was saying that they should go on their holiday alone and enjoy time as a family. Just days later our Michael suddenly and unexpectedly passed away and they immediately felt sure that we were meant to join them.

And so it was that, on Mark's first birthday without his son, we found ourselves walking down a beach-town boardwalk in a foreign country, still stunned by the event that brought us there.

✱ ✱ ✱

When Michael was fourteen years old, he put together a music video on the computer. He chose the song: *I Am Free* by the Gospel music group *Newsboys*. It was so good that I wondered if he'd like to work in video editing someday.

Perhaps Mike may have even joined with our own organisation's news and information service. I encouraged Mike to think about a media course at the college down the street after finishing his GCSEs at school.

When the song got to the line: *"I am free to dance,"* Mikey had videoed himself behind closed doors using his sister's webcam. It was so uncharacteristic of Mike to dance at all, much less to dance for the Lord! He was so quiet and so reserved. Even to the day he died we never heard Mike sing at all. So he would certainly not dance!

One time, I asked Mike what he'd like from his time at music school where he'd been accepted for a guitar course. He said he wanted to learn how to sing. At first I wondered if that was a typical teenage response that actually meant: "Hello! I'm signed up for a guitar course!" But his face didn't seem to show that this smart remark had crossed his mind. So I decided to take him seriously.

That being so, it was amazing! If this was his extrovert younger sister, I would understand it. But coming from Michael, it was a real surprise.

When we went to his open day at his music college, I asked if it was possible to learn to sing if you're signed up for another music stream. They said they'd work around it if possible. I commented on this response to Mike as we drove home. It actually made sense that Mike would *want* to worship with his voice and with words while playing the guitar. It seemed now that he would have liked someone to help him break out of the cage he was clearly in.

He certainly would only dance behind a closed door! But this homemade music video, compiled when he was fourteen, was so well timed and so brilliant (with his little jig caught on film) that I laughed out loud. I immediately wanted a copy!

We didn't get a copy. He lost the links and didn't redo it. In fact, he never put together another slide show like it.

In the aftermath of his departure, the police had taken Mike's computer, video camera and mobile phone. In a phone call some time later, we were told that these would be kept until after the coroner released them. It would be another couple of months before we'd find out what he'd saved to either of these devices. Strangely enough, we hadn't heard that *Newsboys* song *I Am Free* sung in a church meeting. We only knew it from Mike's video presentation put together.

So it was with profound amazement, while we were walking along the boardwalk just three short weeks after Mikey died, that we came across this very song being sung by a girl with an amp in a make-shift worship service so far from home! We couldn't have timed it so uncannily even if we'd tried!

It was our first morning at our friend's beach apartment and Mark couldn't find the coffee filter papers. That hiccup had delayed our walk out that morning. In the seven days we were there, there was only one Sunday morning when church meetings were held at the beach hall a few hundred metres down the boardwalk.

The duration of most songs is about five minutes, so the window of opportunity was incredibly tight. Had we walked in the opposite direction we wouldn't have heard the song. Had we hit that section of the boardwalk five minutes earlier, we would have been far enough past the music hall to no longer be able to hear it when it started.

This was Mikey's song. It was the first he'd put together using computer media — and the only one we saw him dance to. Had we left the apartment five minutes later, we wouldn't have been outside that music hall when they began to play it. The chances were incredibly slim for hearing it at all!

★ ★ ★

Straight after Mike's Celebration of Praise (funeral) service, his sisters went to a youth camp in Holland. Mike and his sisters were all booked in to go on this annual adventure together. As it turned out, the first day of camp was the day of Mike's funeral. We had thought of cancelling this trip for the girls. But having thought of the options (and with their own unique needs for processing their loss as young people would), we felt it best for them to go on as planned. They would need to be among their close friends and youth leaders at this incredibly difficult time.

While there, Akíla had several multi-layered questions in her search for understanding the loss of her only brother. To one small group of friends she asked, "When it comes to forgiveness and we are to forgive anyone who hurts us, has anyone thought of forgiving God?" Her friends were clearly undecided and couldn't think that a perfect God would do anything wrong to begin with. Therefore He can't be in a position of needing our forgiveness.

She left it at that, but it was playing on her mind as she grappled inside with grief's great hurt. But on the night before we flew out for this beach-town break, Akíla told us what happened around the camp fire. In tears over her hurt, along with the concept of forgiving, or not forgiving God, she decided to cross the fireside circle and speak with the camp leaders.

As she approached, and before she could speak her mind, her camp leader said, "I'm glad you came over. I've been wanting to come over to you because I think God has three things to say to you:

First, Mike knew you all loved him." This was a topic Akíla had struggled with from the first day. She mentioned it in her speech at Mike's funeral.

"Secondly," he said, "I think God wants to say He's sorry for the pain that He has caused you." This was the second issue Akíla had struggled with, but had so far received no answers for.

"And lastly, Mike's dancing. In fact he's so caught up in dancing he doesn't realise he's gone!"

✶ ✶ ✶

Again in tears as we walked through the mist brought to shore by Hurricane Bill, Mark and I were blown away. Here, in this foreign land, and on the very first morning, the first thing we heard was Mikey's song. A song we'd spoken of so much over the last couple of weeks, yet were certain we'd probably never find a copy of again — not in the way Mikey had assembled it.

As we stood outside that music hall on his first birthday without his son, Mark heard: "Happy Birthday Dad."

He hadn't received any presents or even a card from us for his birthday, but as he stood there it was as if Father God had sent the best present Mark could have asked for: the message that Mikey was free. He is freed from the shell that seemed to hold him in.

Mike was now free to be all that God wanted him to be and all what he was designed to be ... free to run ... free to dance.

This *breadcrumb* from the hand of God nourished us once again and restored our hope in His controlling power, authority and extraordinary timing. Even in a far-off country, the *breadcrumbs* kept falling from the sky.

To say that stumbling so perfectly across this song in a foreign beach town was simply a well-timed *coincidence*, would be just like rejecting God's Grace — His loving kindness generously poured out. Through all these moments, we've discovered for ourselves that God's love is better than life and because of this, our lips *will* praise Him.[50]

18. KUTLESS

It was the second morning of our recovery break away and we were peddling along in a peddle car with our friends, Todd and Karen. We were heading down the beach boardwalk to find breakfast when we came to the exact spot where we heard the song *I am Free* the day before. We found there yet another surprise in store for us. The Gospel rock group *Kutless*, were set to play at the small beach-town music hall that night!

★ ★ ★

When our Michael fell backwards six metres from the top of a climbing wall, he was convinced he'd be in a wheelchair for the rest of his life. Thankfully, he was discharged from the hospital the next day. But this injury just after his sixteenth birthday caused him to be off school for three months. While recovering, Mike picked up his Dad's old guitar and went onto the Internet looking for the latest Gospel music.

We had no part in the forming of Mike's music likes and dislikes. He knew all the groups out there and gravitated to some more than others. The first *Kutless* CD he bought was at *TeenStreet*[51] in Germany later that same year. The first *Kutless* song he liked and showed to me (no doubt because of the brilliant guitar pieces in it that I also enjoyed) was *Take me In* from their *Strong Tower* album. Amazingly, this was one of my favorite songs from some time back. The way this particular song was played by them was totally brilliant!

With parents from two countries, I asked Mike one day where he felt he belonged: in England or Australia?

His reply surprised me. He said that he would have more opportunities in America or Australia. But America had not entered into any of our previous family discussions! Mike also wasn't an opportunist. Nor was he a career-orientated person. To answer this way, I knew he only meant 'opportunities to be involved in large-scale worship'. On the Internet he would have seen the big churches and large Gospel music events in those two countries.

By mid-2007, Michael heard that *Kutless* was holding a competition for young guitarists. The winner would get the privilege of playing with them — Mike was excited!

To this day, though, I don't think he applied. It was simply a thought and dream that propelled him into a vision of his future that would find him involved in large-scale worship. It was a dream that never left him, but kept him focused to save madly for his music school training in Coventry that was due to start September 19th.

Mike died 50 days in sight of his dream.

✱ ✱ ✱

As we paid for the *Kutless* tickets at that beach-town box office just three short weeks after Mike left us, we couldn't believe that we were about to see Mikey's favourite group! It was a group that Mike followed but had never been able to see them in concert.

Mark mentioned our story to the lady at the box office. He told her why we were there so far from home in the first place. Then, how amazing it was to be seeing *Kutless* just over three weeks after Michael died … She was in tears.

Later that day our friend, Todd, asked me about going to the concert early to see if we could meet the band in person. Mark was thinking the same thing as we got ready for dinner. As the evening moved on though, we arrived only in time to be seated. Todd went backstage regardless of the show time and emerged with the message that they already knew about us and wanted to see us! Apparently, they had received a note and wanted to meet us. It seemed that the lady from the box office had already told them.

We got some lovely photos taken with the group before they went on stage. During the evening they played *Take Me In* — my favourite song, and the first *Kutless* song Mikey asked me to listen to on his MP3 player back when he was sixteen. After the show the girls bought the last poster that the group had signed and the last T-Shirt in their size. Framed in Mike's room now are a couple of really cool photos that were taken with the band members that night.

Mike wouldn't have been at all jealous. He would have smiled broadly if God was to tell him. He'd be glad we got this blessing, knowing it was *his* group that we were seeing.

Kutless had just come off an international tour which included places like Australia and Canada. They played for audiences of thousands.

This, on the other hand, was a small family beach town — an island on the New Jersey coast and cut off from the mainland by marshlands. It was such a traditional, family-oriented town that no alcohol was served anywhere. It was the first time that the local college and Christian radio station had managed to get a Gospel music group to play at that thousand-seat music hall. They only sold 400 tickets that night. It must have been the most sedate concert *Kutless* ever had! And it came in one single 24-hour window of opportunity when we were there.

Had we not gone to breakfast in that direction that morning, we wouldn't have seen the sign up. There was only one event per day in that small music hall, and the signs are renewed each night. By the next morning, Mark noticed that there was already another sign up for the next artist. It was a one-off show and an impossibility to plan such a coincidence.

Standing in that beach-town music hall just three weeks after Mikey died, I looked down the row of chairs at Mark and the girls. They were clapping and dancing as if on Mike's behalf. These were songs sung by a band that Mike followed for the last two-and-a-half years of his life, yet hadn't seen himself. Through the lyrics that they wrote, this band inspired Mike to worship his Maker and to aspire to become like them.

In that instant, I couldn't help but thank God for being God. No-one on earth could have arranged so perfectly this unexpected moment. It was as if all of eternity stood still especially for us to experience (and even enjoy) this night in time. It was a snapshot of an unbelievable coincidence that can only be describe now as a God-incident — as He sent us His *Breadcrumbs in this Storm*.

19. FINDING MEANING AMONG THE ROCKS

The girls had left me with all the belongings and Mark had also headed down the beach. I was alone and beginning to sit uncomfortably on those hard rocks. Just as I started wishing someone would come back, I looked up to see a sign that read: *Keep off the jetty.*

I smiled at the Americans calling this surf-breaker and pile of rocks, a 'jetty'. Isn't a jetty flat so that you can tie a boat to it and walk on it? Perhaps you could do some fishing off it ... I didn't move. Instead, my attention was caught by two little sparrows that had just popped up from among the rocks.

"Aw, that's cute," I mused. "There's Mark and I ... how sweet."

Before long, two more sparrows appeared from the rocks below. They sat together on a separate boulder. "That's nice Lord," I whispered. "There are the girls. Now it's just the four of us. It's a shame Mike's missing from our family now."

Just as I said that, out from beneath the rocks came another little sparrow. It sat itself on yet another rock, separate from the others. "Okay God. We do still have Mikey. He's just not with us. He's sitting on another rock, that's all."

Then, quite unexpectedly, a sixth little sparrow appeared! "O my word, Lord. This *can't* be prophetic!" Maybe it's not such a good idea, after all, to find meaning among the rocks!

The six little sparrows flew off together and the next wave rolled in.

20. OVERLOOKING CENTRE COURT

At the end of that 'recovery break away', our oldest daughter was to return to the *Logos Hope* from Newark airport. So, with Hurricane Bill receding but Hurricane Danny approaching behind torrential rain, our friend Todd, offered to take us to New York early. This put us in Times Square on the morning of the fourth Sunday after our Michael left us.

After taking our daughter to the airport, Todd offered to take us to the closest church to where we were staying. However, we arrived late and it was a very popular church. So Mark, Todd, and our younger daughter had to stand at the back but, quite amazingly, one of the ushers found a spare seat for me in the center tiers. And so it was that I found myself seated directly above the stage in that fascinating old, converted theatre of Times Square Church, Manhattan, on the forth Sunday without my son.

I'd only been in a Playhouse theatre once before. I had taken Mark to see a dance group from Ireland for his 40th birthday at a lovely old theatre in Edinburgh. At the time, I remembered marvelling at how steep the tiers were! Everyone had full view of the stage, no matter how high up they were sitting.

Now I was seated in the first of the tiers. A full view of the stage was laid out before me as I stretched forward to see the congregation at ground floor level. It felt like I could reach out and touch that stage. As their choir began to sing, I welled up with tears. For the first time I had a glimpse inside Mike's dream of being part of large-scale worship.

Looking at the stage below me, I wondered if the video clips on the Internet of large churches, like Hillsong Australia, were only filming 'the centre court' — like the well-known tennis Centre Court at Wimbledon Stadium. For the first time, I began to wonder what could be seen if only it were possible for the camera to pan out far enough to take in all of what the angels could see as well.

Would the stage before me be surrounded by tiers upon tiers that extend up and out, stretching into Eternity?

Behind me I imagined the eternal cloud of witnesses[52] also enjoying this remarkable chorale. As my tears flowed, I realised that we hadn't taken Mike to see this sort of thing. He'd never been in a church like this. He only dreamed about it, and quietly wished that he'd one day get the privilege of playing his guitar on a stage like the one below me now.

I whispered an apology to God for not taking Mike to see such diverse worship teams in his lifetime. Yet I thanked God for that unexpected moment as He seemed to convey us through August 2009, as dazed as we were.

I marveled at the concept of everything that is now visible being only a shadow or reflection of the things to come.[53] That being the case, what a marvelous future has Father God planned for His people in Heaven. At that very moment, Mike may even be witnessing something that's even more astounding than this wonderful vision laid out before us in that beautiful theatre.

Closing my eyes and listening to the sweet voices, this became yet another amazing *breadcrumb* of sweet, rich 'manna' to feed on, enjoy, and to soothe my soul, as the winds of change began to roll back the clouds.

21. LEAVING THE WILDERNESS WITH POWER

The speaker stepped to the podium in that beautiful old theatre in Times Square Church, downtown Manhattan. After introducing his message: *Leaving the Wilderness with Power,* his first words were: "Let us be absolutely clear, it is no longer a matter of years but months…"

In tones that echoed the ancient prophet Jeremiah in the Bible, the speaker went on to explain that (at a time when people were pouring out words of prosperity and future hope of financial recovery) he predicted a considerable downturn in the events ahead. While some, who chose not to have a faith in a 'higher order of things', might wring their hands with nowhere to turn, *his* church was to be absolutely prepared.

For the sake of those whom Jesus had compassion for because 'they were distressed and helpless like sheep without a shepherd'[54], the Believers there should be ready to 'lead through the process' — through hard times. Just like Jesus had done in His own experience of 40 days in the wilderness[55], they could then *leave the wilderness with power.*

I sat amazed. I really couldn't believe what I was hearing in light of the horrible 'wilderness' that we'd just entered! My mind wandered onto a phone call I'd received just days after Mikey left. A close friend (who was herself dying of brain tumours) said that I was 'leading her through the process'. It was uncanny — a supernatural coincidence.

In that darkened theatre as the speaker's strong voice pierced the silence, I realised that she was right.

Unbeknown to me, I was taking the lead as I should in matters of life and death and faith as a Believer and follower of the Lord of Life. In Jesus' day, where did people without hope turn, except to those with good news — the "gospel" message — the words of Eternal Life? As it was rightly pointed out to Jesus, "...*you alone have the words of eternal life...*'[56]

Back then there was nowhere to turn. And since then, no-one has come up with the same or better idea. Hope in Eternal Life, in the way that the Bible describes it, is only found in Jesus' teachings.

Our world, as we once knew it, has ended for us and it feels like the end of the world. I'm not saying that this is a precursor to the end of *the* world. That would be incredibly egocentric when there's seven billion other deaths that are just as significant across the globe.

I'm saying that a tornado hit our home. It carried us into the upper stratosphere before dropping us into a foreign country to receive some pretty amazing *breadcrumbs* from the hand of our Creator and Father God.

When a storm brings an end to your world as you knew it, you may run the risk of thinking that it's time for the end of *the* world. So when the main speaker at Times Square Church opened up his thoughts that Sunday morning, I was drawn back to the journey that had brought us to that place.

✱ ✱ ✱

We had been flying over the Atlantic Ocean and heading for Philadelphia on the previous week-end when the plane tipped horribly to one side. Instead of correcting itself, it then tipped wildly to the other and I thought, "This is it!"

The turbulence caused by Hurricane Bill off the coast of America in the summer of 2009 was something I hadn't experienced before in 25 years of air travel. To top it all off, we were using an airline that saw one of their planes crash off the coast of Brazil only six weeks earlier.

We were all together though, the last four in the family now, and Mike had 'gone on ahead' of us. He was gathered like the first fruits of a harvest. Maybe this was what the whole awful event was about after all: it's our time to go now.

The plane didn't crash, but you wouldn't have blamed me for having such thoughts if you knew what my daily Bible readings had been about since Mike left us.

Every day for the last 21 days since Mike's departure, my *QUIETIMES* book led me to chapters in the Bible about impending judgment, and the ushering in of a Saviour King. So if I'd thought that God's timing was perfect to this point, I wasn't so sure with the Bible readings that were covered for the remaining days of August! Surely God would know I should be reading happy passages of sunshine and butterflies, instead of the final act in a global play!

These prophetic books, in the Old Testament part of the Bible, spoke of a physical judgment that actually happened in history to those it was originally written for. But these books also pointed to a future hope 'after the storm'. I was reading the *Book of Joel* Chapter 2 — a Bible passage quoted often these days by Believers — as I sat buckled into my seat while our plane pitched 10,000 metres above the sea.

Many Believers in recent years have looked at v28-29 in this chapter and have hoped for a real move of God's Holy Spirit in our lifetime — where Joel's words would ring true of our own experience today. However, it wasn't until this flight, as I read these words for August 21st, that I realised they were only a tiny fraction of the whole chapter.

The rest of the chapter, with its apocalyptic vision of things to come, wasn't very good for someone whose faith was formed at a time when Armageddon wasn't written off as science fiction (or an event that won't happen for a few more centuries at least). It wasn't a reading that was particularly brilliant for someone who had just lost their only son, and was at that moment travelling on a plane that was about to release its oxygen masks!

As the plane jolted furiously, coupled with the play-back of my own words (that Mike would be part of Jesus' entourage when He returns), the end of *our* world as I once knew it started to look like the beginning of the end of *the* world!

When my mind came back into focus, the speaker at Times Square Church was drawing his thoughts to a close. I wondered how it was possible to truly *leave the wilderness* (those moments of desert torment where there's no water at all for your soul) and to come out of that experience not just as a dried out survivor, but to actually move on *with power*.

Although those past weeks remained a 'black hole', like the vortex of one of those hurricanes that passed us by in the days before that Sunday morning, Father God seemed to feed us with unexpected moments. They appeared to be designed to make us feel better, and one such moment was this one, inside Times Square. With each new moment that we unexpectedly uncovered, I became aware of just how difficult this storm could have been without the help of my Maker who knows me inside out.

I wondered how I would have fared without my Maker's help. Metaphorically, it would be like a plane ride through air turbulence without wearing a seatbelt. Worse still would be to try to walk around in it. I'd be thrown mercilessly about without knowing when the turbulence was expected to end.

The stabilizing calm that came from finding *breadcrumbs* seemed to quieten my soul. One of those unexpected 'treasures of darkness' that we found in store for us in secret places[57], came wrapped in a cardboard box. We brought it back to England with us after this unplanned break in America...

★ ★ ★

Before returning to the UK, Mark bought me an oil painting of a beach scene after a storm. Depicted there are waves that mercilessly buffet the weather-worn rocks. The picture is perfect for two reasons. We'd also just finished a week at a beach town where we experienced firsthand how Hurricane Bill had wreaked havoc in the first half of the week while Hurricane Danny finished the job off by the following weekend! So it illustrates almost exactly what we experienced during that week.

It also portrayed our situation at the time — the metaphoric life-storm that raged over our family — having just survived our own private tsunami. As I look at my painting now, I can almost see the sand being dragged into oblivion.

But the smattering of black clouds are moving away into the distance. The early morning sun has just broken the night and its warm rays illuminate the closest wave.

My painting now hangs opposite me on our lounge room wall as I sit here typing this story to you. I got a small brass inscription engraved for it. I've called it: *After the Storm*. But it wasn't until we unpacked it at home and stood back taking in its full significance for us, that I noticed one more thing.

Taking central place just below the early morning sun, five sea gulls had just taken flight: two together and three slightly separate. In our hearts, we will still always be parents of three children and a family of five. It's just that one of us has now flown away.[58]

As the eye of the storm passes further away, there are still no solid answers. But one thing is sure: in our hour of unspeakable distress, the God who sees us has made Himself known. Now I have seen at work the One who sees me.[59]

22. MIKE'S LAST DAY ON EARTH

July 31st 2009 — Psalm 145: a Psalm of Praise by King David.

This was my Bible reading for Mike's last day on earth:

> "I will exalt you, my God and King;
> I'll praise Your Name forever.
> One generation will declare your works to another
> and I will speak publically about your great deeds.
> The LORD supports all those who fall;
> He lifts up again all who are bowed down.
> The LORD is near to all who call on him.
> He fulfils the desires of those who respect Him;
> He hears their cry; He saves them.
> The LORD watches over all who love Him.
> My mouth speaks praises of GOD.
> Let every creature praise His mighty Name forever."[60]

Even if some may still say that we've imagined everything. Even if some may think that Mike's death was purely and simply a physical event — the machine stopped, that's it and that's all. This event has changed the fabric of our family forever. With all the so-called 'coincidences' surrounding it, we have become convinced without any doubt that the Creator God *hears our cry*. He *watches over all who love Him*, and therefore *our mouth will speak in praise of the LORD*.

— Let every creature praise His Holy Name forever —

23. THE LIFTING OF THE CLOUD

Six weeks after our Michael left us, I went to bed with a tiny sensation within my spirit. It was welling up in excitement.

After getting to what I felt was surely 'the brink of insanity' in the dark hours of the previous night, I'd resolved to grasp with both hands the life that God has given me. I had to focus now on my two amazingly captivating daughters and my wonderful husband. My lovely house (that I had only just finished decorating on July 31st — the night before Mike died) was now waiting for me to enjoy as I surveyed my handiwork. So to help myself to 'rise up again', I had committed to join the gym the next day.

September 8th was to mark the 'lifting of the cloud in the wilderness'.[61] The time of mourning was over. It was time to break camp and move on into the next season. Upon opening my *QUIETIMES* book (and not surprised at all now by the growing coincidences), the reading set for that day was to be taken from the *Book of Acts* Chapter 16 in the Bible.

A full circle had come round from the day I sat quoting Paul's 'jail house story' back to God, before dawn on the third day after Mikey left us. I was praying for a 'jail break' for Mike, in the hope that he may return to us. But this is what I now learnt:

In life's crises humans seem to think more clearly than at any other time. The essentials become essential, the superfluous evaporates, and life takes on a whole new perspective. But why do I often wait until I experience either danger or loss before I get a grip on what's *really* important?

109

In their foxholes, and under enemy fire, many WWII soldiers 'got religion'. But people have since become skeptical of anyone who becomes a Christian under stress. Yet there's many, including the Philippian jailer in this story in the *Book of Acts* Chapter 16, who show that some 'foxhole conversions' are genuine and lasting.

Because of this, I knew that I should be open and sensitive to the One who made me, especially when I'm under stress. It may be that my Maker is trying to help me to become a 'seer' and someone who views the whole of life from a new perspective.[62]

24. PUBLIC HEARING: CORONER'S INQUEST

October 10th — My Bible reading for the day that we divided up Mike's belongings and cleared his room:

"Praise be to ... the God of all comfort, who comforts those in trouble, so that we can comfort anyone who is in trouble with the comfort we've received from God ..."[63]

***

My stomach turned over when I stepped through the lounge room door and saw Mike's face. Mark had put together a number of photos in an album for a friend, which meant that many could be put onto an electronic photo displayer that he had bought in the days after Mike died. The photo displayer shows photos in a continual cycle until it's turned off. This one photo was exactly how we found Mike when he died.

We had been on a car journey to Mike's interview down at the music school in Coventry. Mike had fallen asleep on the way home. He was completely 'out solid in sleep' in the passenger seat when Mark took the photo. I had sat looking at that same face on August 1st, and knew every detail of it. Even the tips of his teeth showing from his slightly open mouth were imprinted on my memory just like that photo, which is now suspended in time. August 1st would be the last time I saw Mike deep in sleep in this way except, on that day, he wasn't asleep at all.

When I stepped through the lounge room door and my stomach turned over when I saw that photo of Mike on the photo displayer, I seriously wondered if it was such a good idea to show it at all, especially at a time like this!

We didn't remove the photo, and the weeks rolled on.

✱ ✱ ✱

The phone rang and I heard Mark say, "Yes, I've been waiting for your call." Before I could start to guess who it was, he said he'd put it on speaker phone so that I could also hear what was being said. Now, two months after the event, this was the call we'd hoped would bring closure for us. With both of us pressed to the hand set, the coroner told us that the tissue samples had arrived back from the toxicology lab down south.

There was nothing found that was unusual or could point toward a cause of death.

With this, and the original autopsy that found nothing wrong with Mike — he was healthy; all his major organs were healthy; there was no apparent heart condition after the cardio vascular system was checked; and no reason to claim a fatal epileptic seizure as the cause — there still remained no provable reason why our boy died.

In the early weeks, helpful friends had sent us newspaper articles and links to Sudden Adult Death Syndrome (SADS) websites, so we asked about this. The coroner's response was that a noted cause of death, such as SADS, would leave clues that point to this conclusion. He went on to tell us that a pathologist's report is as much about what is found as it is about what is *not* found.

With no real 'pointers' that suggest or prove SADS, it would be inappropriate, in this legal process, to put SADS as a cause of death simply by default. In Mike's case, he said that it's better to register Mike's death as "unascertained natural causes", than to say a known medical cause without proof.

To explain this he said that humans are as much an electrical machine as we are a motorized one. The electrics can be tested when someone is alive. However, after the person has lost electrical current (that enables the 'machine of the human' to continue to work), the electrics can no longer be tested. 'Why' and 'how' are impossible to prove after the electrical current ceases.

When the coroner's phone call ended, Mark and I puzzled on.

Another name for electricity is 'power'. When the lights in the house go out we'll often say, "Power cut!" So in the absence of anything wrong with the machine (the pump and system, the 'mechanics of Mike'), the only other thing is the electrics.

But who has created the electrics in the first place?

Every car has an ignition and starter motor that kick-starts the engine — but how does a half-formed human heart start to beat spontaneously in something as tiny as a twenty-two-day old human embryo? The central nervous system can modify the frequency of heart beats, but it doesn't initiate it![64] This initial electrical charge in the first place, along with continual electrical current around the human body thereafter, seems to be a minute-by-minute miracle.

From what I can see, these unexplained phenomena in medical science point only to the power of the Creator. He not only created the human body to work and 'come to life' in the first place, but He *sustains* it miraculously every day:

113

"For in Him we live and move and have our being. As some of your own poets have said, 'We are His offspring.'"[65]

If this is the case then Mike's sustaining *power* (or electrical flow) stopped. In the case of God's sustaining power over human life, Mike's 'power to live' (that bit that seems to be outside natural medical explanation) was *withdrawn*.

Coming back from making another coffee on the morning of that coroner's phone call, Mark opened his Bible to the next Psalm that was due to be read. It said:

"I've thrown myself headlong into your arms — I'm celebrating your rescue. I'm singing at the top of my lungs, I'm so full of answered prayers."[66]

Instead of helping us, it seemed at first to be so out-of-context with what we were talking about and our own personal grief. Why are people so happy in the Bible when my life was falling apart around my ears? Up until this storm, when I thought of enjoying the everyday blessings of life here on Planet Earth, I hadn't realised that I needed to be rescued.

I'm a person with a happy middle-class existence and I haven't had to think of a need to be 'saved'. But when I pass away (even from my lucky middle-class existence), I'm being rescued from work; rescued from the weight of deadlines, the schedules, the responsibilities; rescued from the curse and consequences of sin, from my own basic sinfulness and from tears. I'll be rescued from aging, sickness and disease. I'll be rescued into a place that's far better than here.

Then we realised that, far from losing his future here before he'd reached his full potential, Mike was rescued into something that his Father God had prepared for him. Because of this we will *'sing at the top of our lungs'* that we are *'full of answered prayers'*.

✸ ✸ ✸

After our coffee together, I headed to the office and Mark opened the post. The first envelope held a card from very close friends of Mark's parents. This in itself was amazing as it was now two months since Mike died! But the card reiterated down to the very words everything we'd just been talking about! Two months after the event and, on this day of all days, straight after speaking to the coroner, the words of this dear friend not just confirmed again God's calling on Mike's life but also quoted our own words!

As Mark stood amazed at the timing of the words in this card, a song came on our lounge room CD player ...

> *Only by Grace can we enter, Only by Grace can we stand*
> *Not by our human endeavour, But by the blood of the Lamb*
> *Into Your presence You draw us, You call us to come,*
> *Into Your presence You call us,*
> *And now by Your Grace we come."*

Extract taken from the song 'Only by Grace' by Gerrit Gustafson
© 1990 Integrity Hosanna! Music
(Admin. by Crossroad Distributors Pty. Ltd.)

Just as Mark looked up from the card to focus on the song (with uncanny, precision timing that was little short of miraculous), Mike's face appeared on the electronic photo displayer! It was that same face we saw on August 1st and etched forever in our minds. The same photo that we'd wondered on and off in the past weeks about removing from the photo sequence. The face of Mike fast asleep *on a journey with his father*. Now timed to perfection, it came up on the electronic photo display screen as the words of the song filled the room.

115

With tears flowing now, Mark was in no doubt at all that the Creator God had just clearly spoken. In three instantaneous messages, it seemed that God had clearly spoken to the head of the home and Mike's Dad. He confirmed that what the coroner was saying (and had said in the beginning) was in fact true: there was no *earthly* reason why Michael died. Then in the words on the card coupled with the words of the song, Mike was *called into God's presence and by His Grace Mike came.*

✷ ✷ ✷

Not knowing if we were carrying a genetic defect that caused this sudden death (and therefore would mean that the girls may also be in danger), our GP got all of us swift referrals to a heart specialist on the east coast. The specialist had been recommended to me by the UK charity CRY (Cardiac Risk in the Young), and we attended the clinic soon after. All of us were checked with various heart tests. They also had on file an echocardiogram done on Mike when he was younger. So they were able to re-check this in light of his death.

There was nothing wrong with us. There was nothing wrong with Mike.

Because of this and all the other stories, all earthly reason is laid to rest when it finds its place in heaven.

POSTSCRIPT

Now you've heard my collection of short stories. You may feel that it's a tumble of images. Having been tossed about in the storm currents, these stories will always remain a kaleidoscope of multi-coloured thought.

In many ways, the journey that my family and I have taken is non-transferrable. Most life stories *are* unique. But in telling you this, I'd hoped to leave you with one thought: that the God of Creation is real, He's alive and He's actively involved in the everyday lives of those He created in His own image.

I can't help you to believe this, or any part of what I've written here. You may struggle to believe it's anything but comforting chance. But if the intention was simply to tell you our story, my hope is that you'll walk away knowing that the God who created Heaven and Earth and all things in them, can reveal Himself to you, too. It seems though, that we're to seek Him if we're to find Him, and we're to search for Him with all our heart.[67]

If you would like to seek out the Creator God, I've developed my *Breadcrumbs in the Storm* website www.kathyknight.org The site is for 'seekers' — people who'd like to continue this journey of discovery at a further level still.

Under the tab for *Look Up Books UK* on my website, you will also find my second book: *Mysterious? ...Expect the unexpected...*

If William Shakespeare was right and *all the world's a stage while we are merely players*[68], then my second book covers five decades of scenes that have been played out on a private stage.

The stories in my second book include: a night time escape through the Australian bushland; emerging from a crushed car at the base of a mountain; surviving a shipwreck off the southern tip of South America; a terrorist attack in the Philippines; a near-death experience in Amsterdam; hip-hop in Jerusalem and other exciting adventures.

Although our life stories are ultimately unique and can't be replicated, we have one thing in common: life here on Planet Earth is often shaped by storms. Depending on how we react, we're either moulded positively by them or we're permanently crippled by them. On the whole, we survive most of them and can go on again as before.

But then there's the big one. That one landscape-altering storm that changes forever everything you see around you. It's that one perfect storm where heaven and hell seem to wage a war over you. They're re-forming that inescapable backdrop to the stage of who you will become.

If you survive it and, even more so, if you manage to rise from the ashes victoriously — learning from it, growing stronger inside because of it and most importantly, understand yourself at 'blueprint design level' when you never thought it possible — it could be that everything in your life-play thereafter becomes illuminated by the light of that one defining moment.

END NOTES

[1] Scripture paraphrased from *The Message*. Copyright © 1993, 1994, 1995, 1996, 2000, 2001, 2002. Used by permission of NavPress Publishing Group.
[2] Daniel 5:23 (See also Isaiah 45:20)
[3] Genesis 1:26-27
[4] At the Inquest into Mike's death, the Coroner wanted to put Mike's occupation into his official report. We were all at a loss as to what the title would be for someone who cooks meals at McDonalds. The Coroner filed his report having called Mike a "hamburger chef". We thought Mike would have smiled at that ... just as we had done.
[5] Luke 3:22
[6] Isaiah 45:3 [NASB]
[7] Genesis 14:18-20 and Colossians 1:16-17
[8] Psalm 139:13, 16
[9] Daniel 7:10
[10] Matthew 25:6
[11] Genesis 19:16
[12] Genesis 5:24 [NIV] The words inscribed on Mike's tombstone
[13] Ecclesiastes 1:2
[14] Job 38:1 to Job 40:2
[15] 1 Corinthians 15:51,52
[16] Exodus 16 (Referencing v15)
[17] Psalm 63:3
[18] Referring to Job 1:13-22 and 1 Samuel 1:22
[19] 1 Samuel 16:12 and 1 Kings 18:41-44
[20] Isaiah 45:3
[21] Matthew 9:24 [NIV]
[22] Judges 6 onward (and referencing v11)
[23] Joshua 6
[24] Matthew 4:18-22
[25] Exodus 34:6
[26] www.kathyknight.org (See LookUpBooks for recommended books)
[27] Genesis 2:7
[28] Psalm 90:10
[29] Proverbs 1:8-9 [NIV]
[30] John 17:15 [NIV]
[31] Psalm 118:24 [NASB]

[32] Lamentations 3 – various verses [NIV]
[33] Matthew 4:4
[34] Matthew 24:36
[35] Hebrews 9:27
[36] Matthew 27:37 and Mark 15:26.
[37] Job 1:5
[38] John 3:5 [NIV]
[39] Proverbs 1:10-19 [NIV]
[40] John 1:12-13; Matthew 25:21
[41] Psalm 24:3-5
[42] Matthew 28:1
[43] Matthew 27:62 to 28:4 and Acts 16:25-36
[44] 1 Samuel 2:26
[45] Referring to Numbers 11:4-9 and Romans 1:16
[46] http://www.bebo.com/Profile.jsp?MemberId=4759008102
[47] Isaiah 61:3
[48] Matthew 18:22 [NIV]
[49] 1 Corinthians 15:52
[50] Psalm 63:3
[51] http://www.teenstreet.de/
[52] Hebrews 12:1
[53] 1 Corinthians 13:11-12
[54] Matthew 9:36 (See Also: Numbers 27:17 and Isaiah 13:14)
[55] Mark 1:12-14
[56] John 6:68
[57] Isaiah 45:3
[58] Psalm 90:10
[59] Genesis 16:13
[60] Psalm 145 (various verses)
[61] Numbers 9:21-22 (See also Exodus 40:36 and Numbers 9:17)
[62] *QUIETIMES* - Max E. Anders © 1988 Wolgemuth & Hyatt Publishers Inc. Brentwood Tennessee. - September 8th
[63] 2 Corinthians 1:3-4
[64] http://www.sciforums.com/showthread.php?t=51013
[65] Acts 17:28 [NIV]
[66] Psalm 13:5,6 – Eugene Peterson: 'The Message' paraphrase
[67] Jeremiah 29:13
[68] William Shakespeare's *As You Like It*, Act II Scene VII